Dynamic
Computer
Design

Dynamic Computer Design

Jake Widman

NORTH LIGHT BOOKS
CINCINNATI, OHIO

98   97   96   95   94   5   4   3   2   1

Library of Congress Cataloging-in-Publication Data

Widman, Jake.
   Dynamic computer design / by Jake Widman. – 1st ed.
     p.   cm.
   Includes index.
   ISBN 0-89134-495-0
   1. Desktop publishing.   2. Graphic arts–Data processing.
   I. Title.
   Z253.53.W53   1994
   741.6'0285'66--dc20   93-31129
                                                    CIP

Editorial concept by Diana Martin
Edited by Mary Cropper and Poppy Evans
Interior design by Sandy Conopeotis
Cover design by Sandy Conopeotis

This book is dedicated to my son, Liam,
who had the good sense to wait to be born
until after it was finished.

ACKNOWLEDGMENTS

I'd like to acknowledge the contributions of some friends and colleagues to the process of creating this book:

Gail Koffman, for her invaluable research assistance. Without Gail's timely intervention, I think I'd still be on the phone.

Tim Vogt, who convinced me that I not only *could* write this book, I *should* do it.

My editors at North Light—Mary Cropper, for her continued, almost boundless patience as events conspired against my deadlines; Poppy Evans, whose encouragement and assistance with the final stages got me to the finish line; and especially Diana Martin, who long ago (it seems) helped me figure out just what kind of book this was supposed to be.

All the designers featured in the book, for their inexhaustible willingness to participate. I only hope I've done justice to their talent.

And finally my wife, Caryn Leschen, who gave up part of a vacation, sacrificed numerous weekends, and otherwise put up with my spending far too much time "in front of that damned computer." It's done, hon.

INTRODUCTION

When I joined the staff of *Publish* in late 1986, our most advanced publishing workstation was a Mac Plus with a separate full-page, gray-scale monitor. People at parties would ask me what I did, then stare blankly as I attempted to explain "desktop publishing." And DOS devotees scoffed at the idea of running a computer by pointing at pictures in windows.

At the time, I didn't know much about computers; I just knew about type, design and production from the other magazines I'd worked on. Today, that would be like saying you don't know much about compact discs, but you know about the recording industry. Publishing and design are nearly synonymous with computer use, while computer skills have become a prerequisite for many design jobs.

This book showcases the skills of some of the graphic artists who have set the standard for electronic design. Its purpose is not so much to teach esthetic principles, as to describe methods of realizing ideas. The projects illustrate tricks and techniques that any designer can apply to his or her own work.

Most of the designers featured work on the Macintosh—no surprise, given the history of electronic design so far. The Mac isn't a prerequisite for digital designers, however. Most of the Mac programs these designers use—Aldus PageMaker, QuarkXPress, Adobe Illustrator, Adobe Photoshop, Aldus FreeHand, and so on—are now available for Windows-equipped PCs.

In fact, in most cases, you don't even need the specific programs mentioned; in these days when QuarkXPress sports a pasteboard and PageMaker features a tracking editor, programs are differentiated less by features lists than by working styles. I've tried throughout this book to describe the concept behind the technique, so it can be adapted to whatever software you use.

I continue to be dazzled by the vision and innovation of digital designers. Some of the techniques of the designers in this book astonished me with their insight and cleverness. Take them as inspiration, and in the words of a San Francisco newscaster, "Go out and make some of your own."

CAPTURED IMAGES

• • •

Scanning Art and Using It To Produce a Document

Light Source, Inc., was sure it had a winner in its new image-scanning program, Ofoto. What better way to promote it than a book filled with sample documents showing the different uses of a scanner? Such a book would not only show off the capabilities of LightSource's software but would also stimulate potential customers to think about buying a scanner (and scanning software) for their own design projects. Light Source conceived *Worth a Thousand Words* as something that would promote Ofoto as well as the idea of scanning itself.

For Lori Barra Nason, the book was a two-part job. The book itself had to be designed as well as many of the sample documents within it. The people and businesses profiled are real, but most of the documents weren't at the time.

For the book as a whole, Nason set out to design an attractive setting to display the photos and sample documents. Since the software wasn't ready yet, she used traditional production methods in places where she now would just use scanned photos.

Worth a Thousand Words: Scanning for the Real World
Creative Director: Lori Barra Nason/TonBo designs
Designers: Sandra Koenig/ Chuck Routhier
Hardware: Apple Macintosh IIFX, Apple LaserWriter IINT, Apple OneScanner
Software: QuarkXPress, Ofoto
Fonts: Bauer Bodoni, Futura Condensed

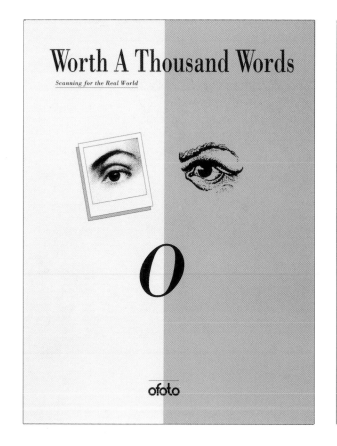

Contents

3

Helping Clients Picture the House of Their Dreams

In the rarefied world in which Brigitte Johns operates, time is indeed money. "My clients are busy people," says the Prudential real estate agent, "and I can't afford to waste their time by taking them to a house that isn't right for them. It's great to show them a picture of the house so that they can decide whether or not to go out in person." Johns can save time for her clients by scanning into her computer professional photos of dozens of homes, and creating a database in which homes are categorized by size, price and various amenities. Clients who visit her office can then look, on screen, at houses that fit their requirements. Johns also prints and sends out customized flyers — targeting clients with homes that may interest them, with personal messages attached. "I even send the flyers to out-of-town clients who are relocating," says Johns. "The pictures are an enormous help."

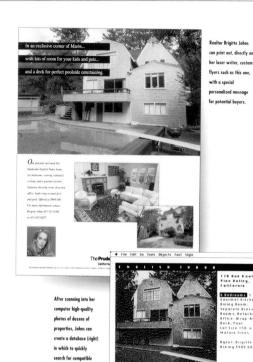

Realtor Brigitte Johns can print out, directly on her laser writer, custom flyers such as this one, with a special personalized message for potential buyers.

After scanning into her computer high-quality photos of dozens of properties, Johns can create a database (right) in which to quickly search for compatible homes.

Prop Keepers Communicate with Clients without Making a Scene

Gray McGee and Josh Koral, the owners of ACME Scenery Company, pride themselves in their eclectic, extensive and ever-expanding collection of props for theatre and film. Such a large and varied collection, however, is hard to keep track of — and just as hard to market. "We want to show exactly what our items look like, and must determine whether an item is in stock," says McGee. "And we need an efficient way to update our list to include new items." With a scanner, McGee and Koral can digitally store photos of each of their 5,000 items, and they can annotate a photo to indicate whether the item is in stock. They can create a general catalog, complete with images and descriptions, as well as custom mini-catalogs for clients who call with specific requests. "For the first time," says McGee, "we'll know exactly where everything is, and customers can see exactly what we have."

A scanned-in logo can be used on the cover of Acme Scenery Company's prop catalog; inside, photographs can accompany descriptions of the items stored in the company's 600-square-foot warehouse. Partners Gray McGee and Josh Koral can also create custom catalogs — complete with scanned-in photos that have been stored digitally and categorized for easy retrieval — for clients who call with specific requests.

Gray McGee and Josh Koral used to track their inventory with a typed list of items, which was sent to potential customers on request. McGee and Koral were available to describe items over the phone, but clients usually found it impossible to settle on an order without visiting the ACME warehouse to see for themselves.

Clip Art in Menus Becomes a Couple's Meal Ticket

At The Avenue Grill in Mill Valley, California, hungry regulars have come to expect a new menu every month — which soon will be illustrated with scanned clip art images from the Dover series of copyright-free books. "We want our customers' dining experience to be a little bit different every time they come in," says Marni Leis, who owns and operates The Avenue Grill with her husband, Joe. "And changing the look of the menu helps keep us fresh as well." Each month, the Leises — neither of whom have any design experience — will scan the images they want into a template created by a designer, manipulating the size and resolution of the drawing as they see fit. They'll then print out the menu on their office laser printer, and take it to a copy shop to run off 200 copies on high-quality paper. The whole process should take no more than an hour, and the cost of these ever-changing menus will probably be no more than $20 per month.

20

With scanned images from the copyright-free Dover book, *Food and Drink—a pictorial archive from 19th-century sources,* Joe and Marni Leis of The Avenue Grill can create distinctive menus. "Scanning has become so easy," laughs Joe, "that even I can do it." The Grill's menus can be printed directly on a laser printer, and reproduced at a copy shop.

Wine labels, food images from clip art books, and The Avenue Grill logo itself can be scanned into the menu by Joe and Marni Leis.

21

Worth a Thousand Words is all about pictures, with a small amount of explanatory text, in keeping with the title. Nason assigned each sample and profile a two-page spread, with the sample document featured prominently on the right page. Placing each sample document on a right-hand page makes it easy for readers to browse through the examples. The supporting material—a photo of the customer, description of the document, and outline of how scanned images were used—is on the left.

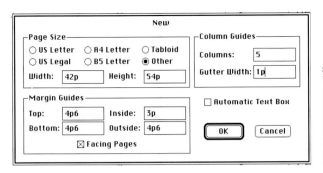

STEP 2: THE GRID

The first step in establishing the page grid was finding the proper size for the block of explanatory copy. Nason wanted only one column of text, less than half the width of the page, since the text was to play a supporting role; but the column had to be wide enough—allow for enough characters on each line—to make the copy comfortable to read. Working mostly in her head, Nason decided on a 3:2 ratio of photo to text column, which suggested a five-column grid. That would allow the main text block on the left page to cover two grid columns, while the captions could fit in one column. To assure herself that this was the best choice, she sketched out some three- and six-column variations. She could tell from the sketches that these grids wouldn't work, so she went with the five-column grid in QuarkXPress. First she set the page size and margins, then the number of columns and the gutter. With those parameters appearing as guidelines on every page, she was able to draw text and picture blocks to size.

Clip Art in Menus Becomes a Couple's Meal Ticket

At The Avenue Grill in Mill Valley, California, hungry regulars have come to expect a new menu every month —

STEP 3: FORMAT TEXT

Even though the explanatory text was secondary to the images, Nason wanted to give it an elegant appearance that would complement the design of the sample documents. She chose Bauer Bodoni Italic because it's pleasant to read and has enough contrast between thick and thin strokes to stand up to the wide leading. To avoid distracting the reader from the sample document on the right, she wanted a headline face that would combine harmoniously with the text face. For this reason, she stayed with the same family for the headline, choosing Bauer Bodoni Roman.

Wine labels, food images from clip art books, and The Avenue Grill logo itself can be scanned into the menu by Joe and Marni Leis.

TRACING TIP: For objects like the handwritten menu categories, you can get smaller, more flexible files if you trace the scan in a program like Adobe Streamline (or any drawing program with a tracing function). That gives you an outline of the object that you can fill with any tint or color, as well as the ability to scale up or down without distortion. The designer didn't do that on the Avenue Grill menu because the featured client didn't have access to a tracing program, and she didn't want to rely on a technique the client couldn't duplicate.

STEP 4: FORMAT CAPTION

The captions needed to fit comfortably into a narrow column measure, so Nason chose to set them in Futura Condensed. This face also creates a good contrast to Bauer Bodoni, giving added color to the page. Its boldness helps the captions stand out and catch the attention of browsers flipping through the book.

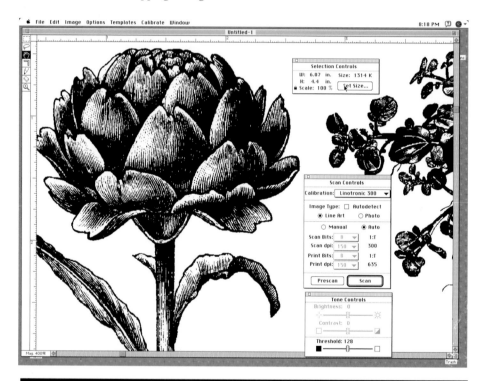

STEP 5: SCAN DOVER BOOK

Scanners aren't just for photographs, as the sample Avenue Grill menu shows. Here, the scanner was used to capture line art—an engraving of an artichoke. All of the pictures on the menu are reproductions of old engravings of food that Nason took from a Dover clip art book, *Food and Drink.* Dover publishes a large line of books containing copyright-free images that can be scanned and used as clip art. Nason scanned the images at 100 percent, scaling them later in XPress.

STEP 6: WRITTEN CATEGORIES

The Ofoto software permits screening to be applied to a black-and-white image; Nason used this technique to create the menu category names: "California Wines," "Appetizers," and "Seafood Grill." She wrote the words with a brush on a separate piece of paper in black ink; then she scanned them and screened them back with the software's Threshold command. Nason scanned the Avenue Grill logo from a photostat supplied by the restaurant the same way, but she left it at full black, with no screen.

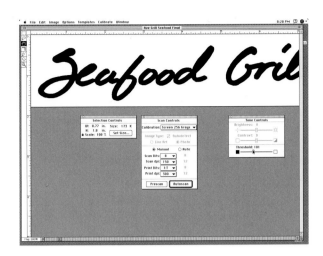

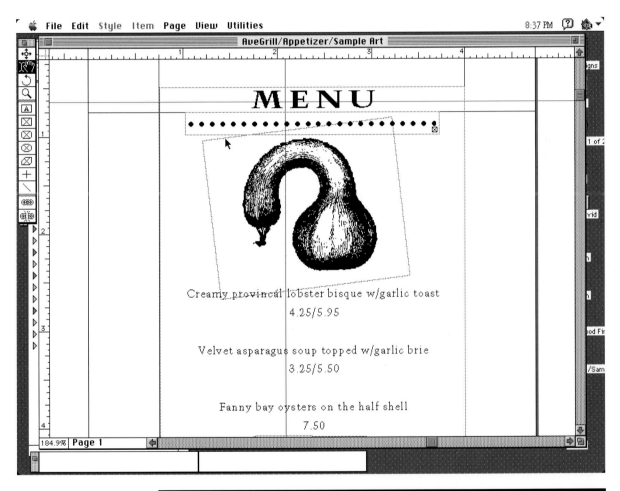

STEP 7: DOTTED LINES

To get the dotted lines, Nason created a text block in XPress the length of the line. She used the program's Tab settings to create a flush-right tab setting and specified the round bullet (Option-8 on the Mac; the command codes vary on the PC, depending on program and interface) as the tab leader character. Tabbing in the text box then creates a line of bullets the length of the frame. For the vertical dotted lines, Nason just rotated the frame after creating the tabbed line.

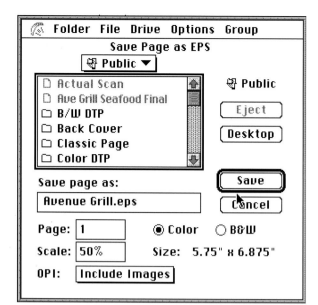

Nason chose to print a mechanical of the menu and have the printer strip it into the book page traditionally. She could have used XPress's Save Page As EPS command to turn the entire menu into a graphic—scaling it as she did so—and then imported it into the book layout. But such EPS files can be very large, to the point where they make a layout difficult or impossible to print. You also have to make sure that whoever is printing your file has access to the fonts in the EPS file as well as the ones in the larger page layout; you may need to send them in a separate file on the disk with your layout.

STEP 9: ADD PHOTO

Nason included a "still life" illustrating the elements that went into the menu design—the Dover book page, the Avenue Grill logo, and some wine labels (used on the back of the menu). She had a black-and-white photo taken of the arrangement and scanned it into the layout to use for position. If she'd been planning to turn the menu into a placed graphic, the high resolution and clarity of the scanned photo would have served for final art. She could have printed the entire XPress page to film with graphics in place.

dfish; & rarely
)—all grilled in the
Lomi salsa,
butter sauce

• • • • • • • •

RILL

Scanner Uses

Scanners are useful to designers for more than just the creation of final electronic art. Other uses—some taken from the *Worth a Thousand Words* book—include:

◆ Scan photos as position-only stats, even if you're going to have your printer make halftones and strip them in traditionally. Use the scans to work out cropping, sizing and placement; then give the printer a printout of the page with the scans in place to remove any doubt about which photo goes where and how it is to be cropped.

◆ Scan physical objects, such as lace, printed fabrics, and plants and flowers to get interesting backgrounds and design elements.

◆ Scan type samples from Dover books and other sources, then trace them in a drawing program to get interesting drop caps and other typographic elements.

◆ Scan a photo and print it on a laser printer for faxing. You'll get a better original than photocopying the photo would give you.

STEP 10: DROP SHADOW

For the drop-shadow effect, Nason tried to create a feathered airbrush tone and save it as a TIFF graphic in Adobe Photoshop. That way, she could import it into a graphics box in XPress and place another graphics box containing the menu on top of it. But when she tried that, she wasn't satisfied with the smoothness of the Photoshop edge. So Nason commissioned a traditional airbrush artist to prepare the drop shadow; since the page was going to be stripped together manually anyway, there wasn't as much incentive to produce everything electronically.

FUNKY APPEAL

◆ ◆ ◆

Creating Art and Custom Lettering

CVS/Peoples Drug is a chain of drugstores with locations throughout the northeastern United States. The company decided to make two brochures the centerpieces of its effort to recruit recent college graduates: one aimed at pharmacists and the other (featured here) for retail personnel. CVS sought out Bernard Hodes Advertising in Boston, a firm that specializes in recruitment ads. Bernard Hodes's creative director, Deborah van Rooyen, wanted a modern, informal brochure to appeal to the college crowd, so she asked Valentin Sahleanu to design a cover in a comic book/Roy Lichtenstein style.

Sahleanu enjoys mixing several graphics programs in his work, and he used a combination of techniques to produce the brochure cover. Van Rooyen had also sketched her idea for the cover logo—involving the word "change" set in a mix of tall, thin type and one handwritten letter—which Sahleanu adapted to the cover. The result is a high-impact brochure certain to attract the attention of potential job seekers.

CVS/Peoples Drug
   Recruitment Brochure
Creative Director:
   Deborah van Rooyen/
   Bernard Hodes
   Advertising
Designer: Valentin
   Sahleanu
Hardware: Apple
   Macintosh IIci, Apple
   13-inch color monitor,
   RasterOps 21-inch
   gray-scale monitor,
   Microtek 600ZS
   color/gray-scale scan-
   ner, Apple Personal
   LaserWriter NT,
   Calcomp color thermal
   printer
Software: QuarkXPress,
   Adobe Photoshop,
   Adobe Streamline,
   Aldus FreeHand
Fonts: Balloon, Futura
   Bold Co

IT'S A CONSTANT AT CVS/ PEOPLES DRUG

CHANGE

STEP 1: SCAN TYPE

Working from Van Rooyen's sketch, Sahleanu set about creating the "Change" nameplate. He couldn't find a computer font that gave him exactly the look he was after, so he turned to Letraset's rubdown type in a face called Bordeaux Roman. He pressed down the letters *CHANG* and scanned the result. He opened the scan in FreeHand, and manually traced the letters.

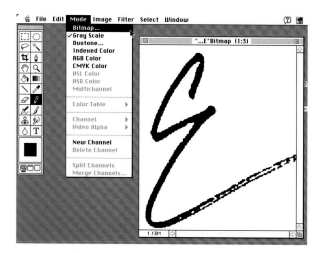

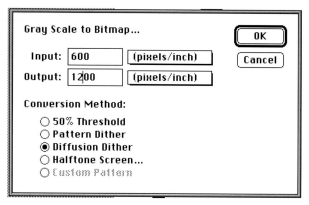

STEP 2: SCAN "E"

For the *E*, Sahleanu first drew the letter several times with a brush on paper. He took the best letter and scanned it as a gray-scale TIFF at his scanner's highest resolution, 600 dpi. He used the Contrast and Brightness adjustments in Photoshop to adjust the lines to the weight he wanted, and then applied the Sharpen Edges filter. After doubling the image's resolution with the Image Size command, he converted it to a bitmap, choosing the Pattern Dither option to get a random, stippled effect. He saved the result as a TIFF file for import into FreeHand.

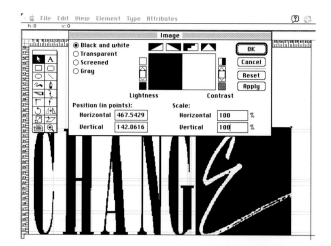

STEP 3: COMBINE LETTERS

Sahleanu next placed the *E* into FreeHand and slid it into position next to the other letters. Since the word would eventually be placed against a black box, he colored the *CHANG* white with FreeHand's Fill command, and also changed the *E* to white on black through FreeHand's Element Info dialog box.

STEP 4: SKETCH ILLUSTRATION

To create the illustration of fearful graduates, Sahleanu started by making several sketches by hand with a fat, black felt-tip marker, working at about 50 percent of final size. His third sketch gave him characters of the proper age and mood.

The Right Tool for the Job

Most computer graphics programs can do a number of different things, but they all have their own individual strengths and weaknesses. If you can, select the best tool possible for the job at hand. For instance, Valentin Sahleanu could have scanned his sketch as black-and-white line art and brought it right into FreeHand to use that program's Autotrace feature. But then he would have had to do all the cleanup of the image in FreeHand. By using Photoshop to perfect the scan before tracing, he got a much cleaner image to work with.

And while FreeHand can automatically trace scanned images, it often gives you curves that follow the traced shape so closely, picking up every rough edge, that you end up with too many points to manipulate efficiently. Streamline is designed specifically for tracing and includes more settings you can adjust—how closely the curve follows the traced shape, or how small a mark to ignore—to make sure the result is just what you want. Sahleanu used three programs where one might do, but he got better results with less work overall.

STEP 5: SCAN SKETCH

Sahleanu scanned his marker sketch at 300 dpi as a gray-scale image so he could use Photoshop's Brightness and Contrast controls to adjust the weight of the marker lines. He also cleaned up random marks and artifacts of the scan. Finally he changed it to a black-and-white bitmap and saved it as a TIFF file for import into Streamline.

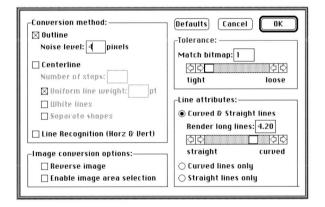

STEP 6: TRACE PICTURE

Next he imported the sketch into Streamline, a program for automatically tracing bitmapped images to turn them into vector graphics. (The vector format would give him the hard-edged, pen-and-ink style he was looking for.) He set Streamline to follow the curves of the scan closely and to produce both curves and straight lines. When the tracing was finished, he saved it in Illustrator 88 format for import into FreeHand.

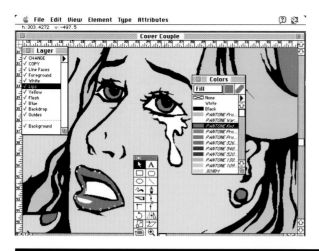

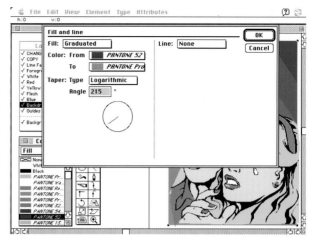

STEP 7: COLOR PICTURE

The traced file opened in FreeHand as a collection of outlines filled with black or white. Sahleanu duplicated most of the paths and set about filling them with color. Duplicating some open paths and joining the ends let him add color within spaces that weren't completely enclosed, such as the woman's teardrop. Duplicating the closed paths also let him trap the image by enlarging the copies slightly to extend under the black areas.

The color on the faces is a very coarse (25 lpi) halftone setting applied to a 30 percent screen of magenta. The imagesetter took care of creating the dot pattern, which imitates the way white skin is colored in comics and Lichtenstein's paintings.

STEP 8: ADD BACKGROUND

For the illustration's background, Sahleanu drew two orange stripes with graduated fills and placed them against a blue field that also has a graduated fill.

STEP 9: CREATE BORDER AND CROP IMAGE

Sahleanu wanted to frame the page with a black border to make the cartoon image stand out and to set off the "Change" logo. For the border, he used FreeHand's Paste Inside feature. First he drew a box with no fill or stroke at the size the image would appear on the page. To crop the picture to fit inside the box, he selected the faces, chose Cut, selected the empty box, and chose Paste Inside. He finished framing the image by creating another box the size of the cover, filling it with black, and moving the illustration on top of it. Finally, he drew a rectangle and filled it with yellow for the stripe at the top.

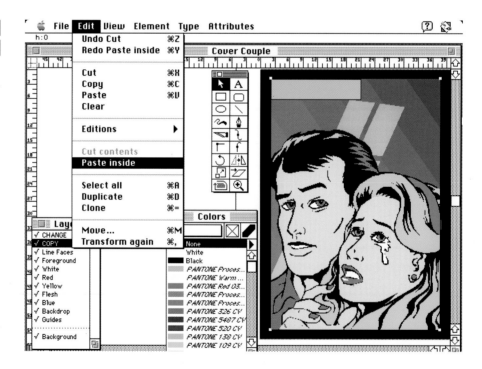

STEP 10: ADD BALLOONS

Because they needed to protrude over the black frame, the word balloons were the last things added to the FreeHand file—they couldn't have stuck out if they'd been in the picture at the Paste Inside step. To create the balloons, Sahleanu used FreeHand's Ellipse tool to draw an oval, then ungrouped it to work on the curve directly. He added three new points and dragged the middle one down to make the arrow.

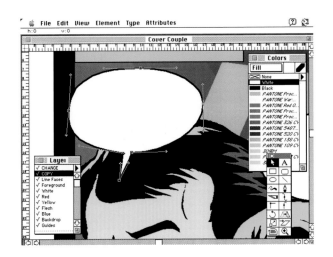

STEP 11: ASSEMBLE ELEMENTS

The cover came together in XPress. Sahleanu set up a transparent graphics box the size of the cover and imported the main illustration. Then he put the dialog and the caption in their own text boxes—formatted in the whimsical Balloon font from Image Club—and positioned them. The "Change" logo was imported into a graphics box with a black background. And last, the "It's a constant..." line was typed in XPress, in its own text box.

WATCHING THE SOAPS.

Who sent John the E-Mai
it? Will Joanne change h
Will Mitch handle the cas
to the b
SOAPS
Program
systems
moving t
linking t
powerful
us all w

WALKING
Merchan
Special
Lighting.
the custo
professio
quality.
family, i
understa

HARVEY
Our CEO, Harvey Rosent
living, breathing leadersh

:.
g shifts. Managing the
nagement
ood head
think on
t, every
you the
yourself,
Peoples.
ssistant
ke over
l of a
3 years.

0% of our
n within.
u'll have
Manager,
r and a
creasing
ewards.

est in a specialized area,
y to find a new job. At

STEP 12: REUSE ELEMENTS

Sahleanu reused the main illustration in other places in the brochure. For instance, the
entire illustration appears on page 3 with new caption and dialog, without the cover logo,
and with a finer halftone for the faces. On the last page, the faces are broken apart and
used separately, a task made easier because they were on separate FreeHand layers.

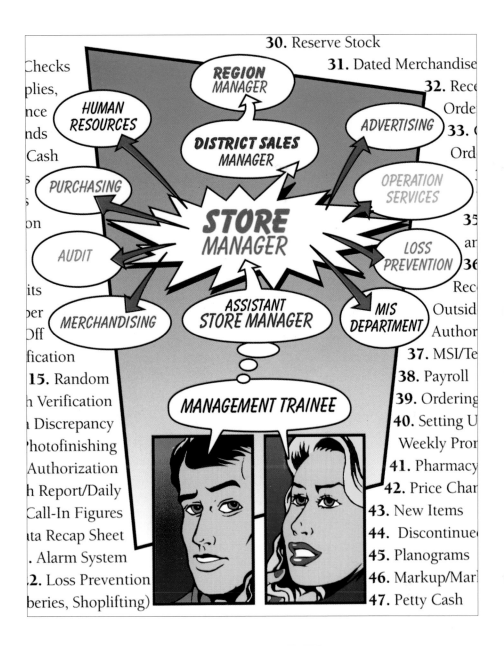

Working With Layers

Many drawing programs, notably Aldus FreeHand and Micrografx Designer, let you assign different parts of a drawing to different *layers*. There are several advantages to dividing a drawing this way:

◆ You can hide all the layers except the one containing the part of the drawing you're working on. That not only removes distracting elements but speeds up your work, since the program only has to display and redraw the detail you're working on. And if you need to redo part of your drawing, you can work on it without having to move other elements out of the way first.

◆ Similarly, you can print out only one or a few layers for proofing purposes.

◆ The ability to print a selection of layers makes it easier to use bits and pieces of your drawing in other contexts, as Valentin Sahleanu was able to do with the two faces in the CVS illustration.

RESTRAINED ELEGANCE

• • •

Effortlessly Exploring Many Different Grids and Type Treatments

The Pacific Telesis Foundation Annual Report documents the philanthropic activities of the Pacific Telesis telecommunications company. The foundation makes grants to community education and arts organizations. Ames's assignment was to improve on the report's existing design without spending a lot of money—the foundation exists to make donations to worthy causes, so its annual report shouldn't look like a lot of the money went to slick paper and four-color printing.

The biggest problem was how to handle the list of grants at the back. The narrow columns used in previous years often forced the name of a recipient organization to run over onto a second line, and readers couldn't easily tell which sum went with which grant. That led to Ames's first decision, made before she even sat down at her Mac: to base the layout on two columns of text.

Since the report is predominantly text, Ames relied on careful typography to achieve the foundation's goal. She decided to give the report a classic look—restrained without being boring, elegant but still a little decorative—that would reflect the fund's cultural and educational activities.

Pacific Telesis Foundation Annual Report
Designer: Monica Ames/ Ames Design
Hardware: Apple Macintosh IIsi, Apple LaserWriter IINT
Software: Aldus PageMaker 4.01, Adobe Illustrator 88
Fonts: Adobe Caslon, Weiss, Univers Condensed Light and Univers Condensed Bold

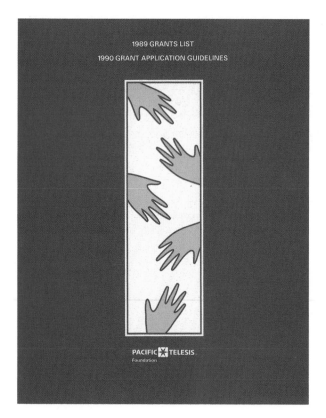

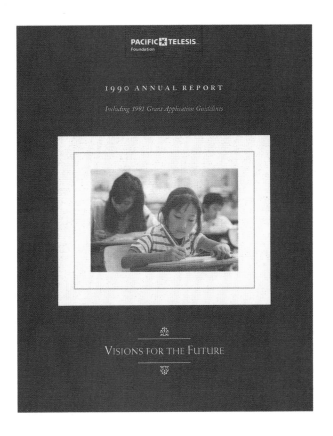

Importing Text With Ease

Like other advanced page-layout programs, PageMaker for the Mac can import text from most of the major Macintosh word processors, and the PC/Windows version of PageMaker accepts files from most PC word processors.

Some tips for importing text:

◆ If you know the type specs in advance, format the text file in a word-processing program before you import it. Text formatting is easier and faster in a word processor, and most page-layout programs can preserve text styles on import.

◆ If you don't know the precise formats, you can still code the text file in advance for the style sheet you'll be using. Most layout programs can read a code like "@BODYCOPY=" (the precise code structure varies from program to program) and automatically assign the BODYCOPY style to the following paragraph(s). That way, all you have to do in the layout program is define the style; if you define it before importing the text, the text will automatically take on the proper format.

◆ If you can't do any preformatting, try using PageMaker's built-in Story Editor. This is a word-processor-like module that lets you edit text and apply styles much more quickly than you can when working on the actual page layout, because the program doesn't bother to reflect your formatting in the Story Editor display.

Ames began by selecting the typefaces, relying on repeated experimentation in a standard two-column grid to narrow her choices. Here PageMaker's style sheets saved her a lot of time. She defined the first treatment that she tried as a Body Copy style, so every time she wanted to try

something new—whether a different typeface or additional leading—all she had to do was redefine the style to change all the text at once.

She finally chose to use only two typefaces—Adobe Caslon and Weiss—for the main part of the report. Adobe Caslon, used for the body text, is a modern interpretation of a timeless oldstyle face; it's traditional without being stuffy. Weiss, used for the titles ("Organization and Purpose"), is a classy face with a chiseled appearance, much favored for documents like annual reports because of its air of serious sophistication. Together, these typefaces strike the note of restrained elegance Ames was looking for.

Ames built on the typographic scheme with some design elements she adapted from old-fashioned book design. The justified text, opening paragraphs set in small capitals, and titles set in caps and small caps all contribute to the classical feeling she was after.

INTRODUCTION

OR THE PACIFIC TELESIS FOUNDATION, 1990 WAS A YEAR OF STEADY GROWTH AND CONSISTENCY. IN ITS SIXTH FULL YEAR OF GRANTMAKING, THE FOUNDATION DISTRIBUTED $7.6 MILLION IN GRANTS, INCLUDING PART OF A SPECIAL $1.1 MILLION GRANT FOR EARTHQUAKE RELIEF WHICH CARRIED OVER FROM 1989. SINCE IT WAS ESTABLISHED IN LATE 1984, THE FOUNDATION HAS AWARDED $35 MILLION IN GRANTS. ABOUT 90 PERCENT OF ITS GRANTS ARE MADE WITHIN CALIFORNIA AND NEVADA.

The choice of Adobe Caslon opened another source of typographic design elements: ornamental figures, which Ames used to set off drop caps and to bracket the captions. As one of Adobe's line of Expert Collection fonts (which includes Minion and Adobe Garamond), Adobe Caslon comes with a wide assortment of extra characters. In addition to the ornaments, the font includes special capitals for titles, elaborate swash caps and true small caps.

STEP 3: TYPE FOR THE LISTINGS

To fit all the grant listings onto a few pages while keeping them legible, Ames turned to a third typeface—Univers Condensed. This sans serif face is a frequent choice for lists, captions, and any other situations that require fitting a lot of text into a small space without crowding. Univers has more personality than the overused Helvetica and offers a variety of weights and styles. She chose Univers Condensed Light for the descriptions and Univers Condensed Bold for the titles.

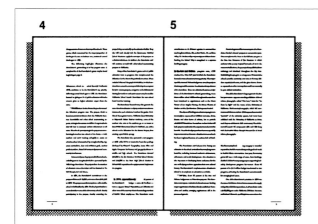

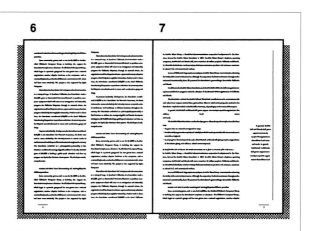

STEP 4: FINALIZING THE LAYOUT FOR THE PHOTO PAGES

With the type treatment decided, Ames next started refining the page layout for the pages with photos. She knew how many pages she had to work with for the entire publication, and she had a sense of how the report had to be divided, since the grant listings were to start on a spread. Printing out the copy in Adobe Caslon, at the point size and leading she'd decided on, gave her a good idea of how much page space she'd have to allot for introductory text and how much she could use for photos and graphic elements. As she did with the type treatment, Ames just created a series of layouts on her Mac, printing each one out—in thumbnails and at full size—to see how she liked it.

than $2 million in the first five years, comprises the largest single investment in the Foundation's history.

The continued emphasis on the Education for the Future Project was accompanied by an increase in funding to arts education programs responding to the disappearance of music and art in public schools. These grants, which accounted for the major proportion of funding in the arts and culture area, continued a trend that began in 1989.

The following highlights illustrate the Foundation's grantmaking in its key program areas. A complete list of the Foundation's grants may be found beginning on page 8.

EDUCATION

Education, which received about $2.7 million in 1990, continues to be the Foundation's top priority. Following a trend that began in 1989, the Foundation focused its giving on K-12 public education while the amount given to higher education stayed about the same.

The Education for the Future Project dominated the Education program area. The project, which is based on recommendations from

The California Child Care Resource and Referral Network has become the state's preeminent source of licensed child care providers.

the California Business Roundtable and other school restructuring reports, is designed to create a model for change in schools that will lead to increased student achievement in all areas. The schools participating in the project are transforming themselves into schools of the future — with teachers and staffs working collegially to create an effective school characterized by strong leadership, vigorous curriculum, clear and ambitious goals, teacher professionalism, shared influence and parent and community involvement.

In its second year, the project added four schools, including one in Long Beach which is sponsored by the Wells Fargo Foundation. The project drew the attention of educators across the nation and was featured in *The Wall Street Journal* and *Fortune*.

In 1991, the Foundation's commitment to the project will rise to $750,000, an increase from $612,350 in 1990. The project coordinators plan to add a middle school in Oakland for the 1991-92 school year that draws its students from one of the elementary schools already participating in the project, thereby extending the project's impact vertically up the education ladder. They also will work closely with the Sacramento Unified School District to apply the concepts of the project on a district-wide basis. In addition, the Foundation staff will continue to work with other school restructuring projects in California.

Many of the Foundation's grants to K-12 public education went to programs that complemented the Education for the Future Project's reform efforts. These included National Geographic's KidsNet, in which students from across the country are linked up via computer for joint science projects, and grants to the Educational Testing Service for an authentic assessment pilot and the California School Boards Foundation for new school board member training.

The Foundation focused many of its grants in the area of teacher education and preparation in an effort to increase the pool of talented teachers for grades K-12. One of these grants went to California State University at Hayward's Urban Teacher Academy; some of the teachers who train at the academy go on to intern at Brookfield Elementary School in Oakland, one of the schools in the Education for the Future Project, thus creating a profitable synergy.

The Foundation also sponsored a new program in 1990 called GTV, an interactive laser disc package developed by National Geographic, Lucas Film and Apple Computer for history and geography classes in middle and high schools. The Foundation donated $25,000 to the San Francisco Unified School District and $56,000 to the Kern High School District in Bakersfield to purchase the equipment and implement the program.

UNITED WAY

In 1990, approximately 35 percent of the Foundation's budget — some $2.7 million — went to support United Way activities in California and other areas of the country where there are large numbers of Pacific Telesis employees. The Foundation made contributions to 51 different agencies in communities reaching from Atlanta, GA, to Fort Worth, TX, to Grass Valley, CA. Traditionally a major recipient of Foundation funding, the United Way is recognized as a separate funding category.

ARTS AND CULTURE

In the Arts and Culture program area, 1990 marked the first full year in which the Foundation focused on arts education as its top priority. The majority of the Arts and Culture

budget was aimed at projects that integrated the arts into the educational experiences of K-12 students. Since arts education became a major thrust of the Foundation's cultural grantmaking, more than a million school children throughout the state have been introduced to organizations such as the Music Center of Los Angeles County, the Dance Theatre of Harlem and the San Francisco Shakespeare Festival.

The object of funding arts education programs is not simply to expose school children to music, dance, theatre and other forms of culture, but to provide educational materials to the teachers and staffs that will both prepare students for the experience and extend its benefit. These kinds of projects have become especially important at a time when arts education in most schools has been neglected because of a serious lack of funding.

The Foundation staff believes that having arts education in the school curriculum has many long-term benefits, including increased academic achievement, self-esteem, and social development. Arts education is also important in developing future audiences for the arts and helping

School children at Brookfield Elementary in Oakland learn about good health habits and AIDS by watching "Thumbs Up for Kids" video.

4

5

STEP 5: THE GRID

The result of all this experimentation was a basic five-column grid that had room for two blocks of text plus one narrow column for captions and white space. The grid also permitted photos and sidebars to extend across three columns.

Even with the grid, the layout continued to evolve as Ames thought of new ideas—ideas as basic and simple as centering the two columns of text on the opening page. That inspiration led to other design decisions that showed up throughout the book—centered text on the inside covers, centered heads over the listings, and so on.

Spot Colors in PageMaker

To create spot colors in PageMaker:

1. Define your spot color, or use one that already exists in the Color Palette. On a color system, it's nice to try to create a match on screen for the printed color, but it's not necessary. (See the color tip on page 23.)

2. Apply the spot color to objects on your page by selecting the object with the Pointer tool, then clicking on the color name in the Color Palette.

3. For colored text, select the text with the Text tool and then click on the color name. You can't use PageMaker's Fill tool to create screened text, but you can create it by defining a tint with the Define Colors command and then applying it with the Text tool.

4. Click Options in the Print dialog box, check the Spot Color Overlays box, and select the colors you want to create overlays for.

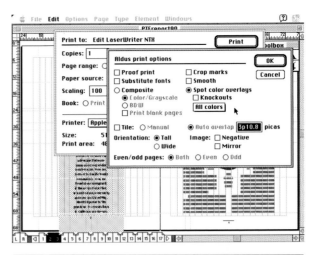

STEP 6: PLANNING COLOR

Desktop publishing programs haven't quite solved all the problems of preparing color pages for color printing. This annual report used only two colors (red and black) in various tints, but even so, it still required ingenuity on Ames's part to make sure they printed correctly. She used a combination of computerized and traditional techniques to achieve the effects she wanted.

COLOR TIP: A color monitor is nice for getting an idea of what a color's going to look like on the page, but you don't need a color system to make spot color separations. Your mechanical's going to be black and white anyway, so all you want PageMaker to do is print the correct elements on each overlay. You can define your spot colors however you want in the Define Colors dialog box—or, for that matter, just use PageMaker's existing colors in the Color Palette. So long as your spot color has a name other than Black, White or Paper, if you check Spot Color Overlays, PageMaker will print the objects you assign that color to on their own sheets.

STEP 7: SPOT COLOR OVERLAYS

On pages where the two colors didn't touch, or where one printed solid on top of a tint of the other, she printed separate overlays for each color. First, she defined the red color, which added it to the Color Palette. For the tint, she applied a 20 percent screen to the red with PageMaker's Fill command. Then, under Options in the print dialog box, Ames chose to print Spot Color Overlays to create two pieces of film—one with the red elements, one with the black. She also gave the printer a composite black-and-white proof of the entire page, along with notes explaining the color divisions, to eliminate any chance of confusion.

1990 GRANTS LIST

STEP 8: SPECIAL CASES

Even when Ames supplied two pieces of film, the printer sometimes had to make some further modifications—for instance, when Ames reversed a word out of a screened colored box (as on the "1990 Grants List" heading). If she simply reversed the type out of the tinted box on the red film, the type would have a ragged outline from the dots in the screen used to create the tint. To get a sharp edge on the type, she had to create a solid black box exactly the size of the screened box, and reverse the type out of the black box instead. The red film, then, contained all the red type, the rules, and a full-bleed screened red box; while the black film contained the rest of the type and a black box with "1990 Grants List" reversed out of it. The printer took care of making a composite film with the type knocked out correctly.

EDUCATION

The California Child Care Resource and Referral Network has become the state's preeminent source of licensed child care providers.

Education, which received about $2.7 million in 1990, continues to be the Foundation's top priority. Following a trend that began in 1989, the Foundation focused its giving on K-12 public education while the amount given to higher education stayed about the same.

The Education for the Future Project dominated the Education program area. The project, which is based on recommendations from

Ames knew that all the photographs would be stripped in by the printer, so on the pages with photos, she didn't bother making the separations herself. Instead, she printed the entire page on one sheet to make a mechanical and included instructions to the printer on an overlay to indicate which elements were red, and used keylines on the page to show where the photos should go.

FOCUS

EDUCATION FOR THE FUTURE PROJECT

The final color production problem arose on those pages where screens of the two colors butted against each other, as on the top of page 11(shown here). Since PageMaker doesn't do trapping, in those cases she produced a black-and-white mechanical. On an overlay, she instructed the printer, who has time-tested ways of handling trapping, what to do with the colors.

Drawing a Pie Chart

To create the graph on page 3 of the annual report, Ames turned to Illustrator 88, an older version of the popular drawing program from Adobe. The current version has a special graphing tool that makes pie charts automatically, but the technique Ames found is still useful with other drawing programs.

The final graph is made up of a tinted circle, with four tinted wedges outlined in white, arranged on top of it. First Ames drew the base circle and duplicated it, positioning the duplicate on top of the original. Then she drew one radius and used Illustrator's Rotate tool—clicking the Copy button each time to make a new radius—to place other radii around the circle. She converted the percent value for each wedge to degrees of a circle (for instance, 35 percent equals 126 degrees) and used those figures for the amount of rotation.

Then she used the scissors tool to cut the circle into arcs and join them to the radii on either side. That created closed wedges she could tint darker than the original circle. The final graph was saved as an EPS file for import into PageMaker.

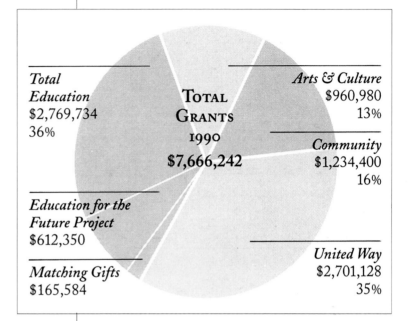

Total Education
$2,769,734
36%

TOTAL GRANTS 1990
$7,666,242

Arts & Culture
$960,980
13%

Community
$1,234,400
16%

Education for the Future Project
$612,350

Matching Gifts
$165,584

United Way
$2,701,128
35%

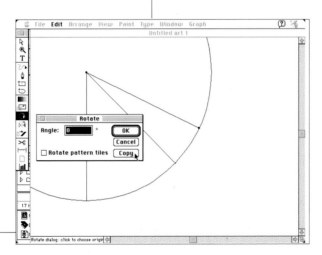

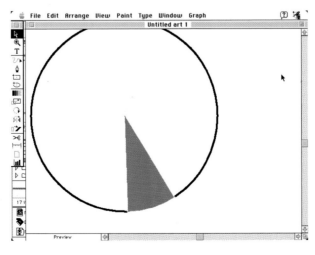

CLASSICAL STYLE

◆ ◆ ◆

Designing a Logo and Applying It To a Stationery System

Hella Tsaconas is a wardrobe consultant: She'll visit your house and come shopping with you to make sure your clothes are well-coordinated and flattering. That kind of service calls for a business card and stationery that project a distinctive sense of style. Before she called Monica Ames, though, Tsaconas was using the kind of off-the-shelf business card you order at an office supply store.

Most wardrobe consultants rely on feminine imagery—flowers, pastel colors—but Tsaconas wanted to avoid stereotyping her customers. She asked Ames for a design that would appeal to men as well as women.

Ames started with her own sense of Tsaconas's personal style—a classic look that relies on clean lines and solid, bold colors. Building on that idea, and taking into account Tsaconas's Greek ancestry, Ames decided to work with angular elements that recall ancient Greek patterns without obviously copying them.

*Hella Tsaconas
    Stationery*
Designer: Monica Ames/
    Ames Design
Hardware: Apple
    Macintosh IIsi, Apple
    LaserWriter IINT
Software: Aldus
    PageMaker 4.01, Adobe
    Illustrator 88
Font: Weiss, custom
    version of Empire

Designer and client had agreed that the basis for the business identity should be a small stamp or icon that could be used on stationery as well as a business card. Ames decided to start work with Tsaconas's initials, since both *H* and *T* are angular letters made up of straight lines. Lines elsewhere on the card would pick up the angles of the letters.

Ames started by experimenting with the form and position of the letters in Illustrator 88. She looked for a tall, elegant typeface to represent Tsaconas's personal style and found Empire, a sophisticated face with an Art Deco feel, in a type sample book. Looking closely at the details of the letterforms, she drew a shorter version of them in Illustrator. The *H* and *T* are such simple shapes, drawing them freehand was easy.

EMPIRE

A B C D E F G H I J
K L M N O P Q R S T U
V W X Y Z & $! ?

1 2 3 4 5 6 7 8 9 0

TYPEFACE TIP: Thousands of typefaces have been designed over the years, becoming more or less popular according to the fashions of the times, and many of them haven't been digitized for use by desktop publishers. That doesn't mean you can't use them, however. If you can find a printed sample, in a type sample book, an old magazine or wherever, you can scan and trace it in a drawing program, or just attempt to reproduce it freehand.

If you do this in a program like Altsys Fontographer for the Mac or ZSoft's Publisher's Type Foundry for the PC, you can turn your drawings into a true font that you can type with. Or, you can use a program like Altsys's Art Importer or CorelDRAW's WFNBoss utility to turn groups of drawings into fonts. This is all legal as long as you don't attempt to sell the font under the same name as you found it.

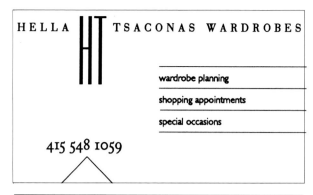

HELLA TSACONAS WARDROBES

wardrobe planning

shopping appointments

special occasions

415 548 1059

STEP 3: STACK THE TYPE

The next problem was how to position the letters in relationship to one another. Once again, the letterforms themselves suggested the arrangement: in Empire, *H* and *T* are vertically symmetrical and the same width, so it worked to stack them on top of each other. Other arrangements were considered, but none accomplished Ames's goals as well as a simple stack.

HELLA TSACONAS
WARDROBES

wardrobe planning
shopping appointments
special occasions

4 1 5   5 4 8   1 0 5 9

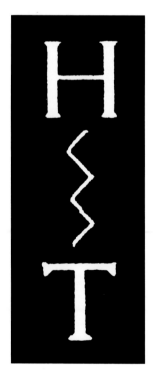

STEP 4: ZIGZAG LINES

All the while, Ames was also working with a zigzag line that would reinforce the angularity of the logo and suggest classical Greek design. The line, rendered in Illustrator, has a hand-carved look because the width of the line varies subtly—even the wide parts aren't the same width the whole way. Ames tried placing the line differently when she was considering other typefaces, but once she stacked the Empire letters, a vertical border seemed like the obvious solution.

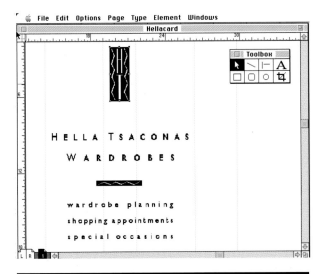

STEP 5: TRANSFER TO PAGEMAKER

Ames brought the finished logo into PageMaker to work on the type for the rest of the business card. At the time, PageMaker offered much better control over type formatting—kerning, justification, and so on—than did Illustrator. Since version 3.0, Illustrator has dramatically upgraded its type-handling capabilities, and now Ames could easily finish the project in Illustrator.

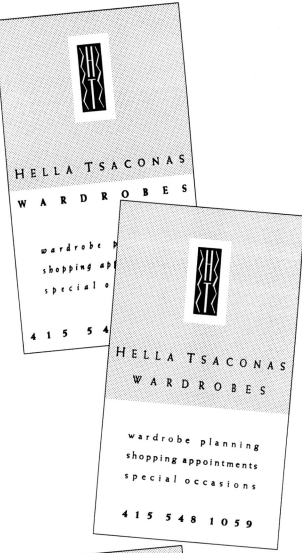

STEP 6: TYPE TREATMENTS

Ames considered several typefaces for the material on the business card, including the graceful Adobe Garamond Italic and Gill Sans, a sans serif face with a warm, human feeling. But it only took a few printed experiments for her to narrow the choices to two: Bauer Bodoni, which would go with Empire because of its strong vertical stress, and Weiss. Weiss is a "transitional" face with small, triangular serifs; as such, it looks simpler than many serif faces, which recommended it for use with the simple, geometric stamp. Ames sent three type treatments for each face to her client.

Tsaconas chose a design that used Weiss; it also happened to have the zigzag in a horizontal bar, so Ames kept that element as well.

COLOR TIP: Since the Hella Tsaconas job would be printed in only one color, the designer worked in black and white and told the printer which color ink to use. If you want to see the colors on screen, however, you must do some planning. For an imported element like the *HT* stamp to show up in color in a layout program, you must color it in the drawing program beforehand. Then you can define the same color in your layout program and use it for elements created there. The two colors will look at least similar on screen.

If you're planning to do four-color separations from your layout program, you have to define the color in terms of process colors—not by Pantone or any other system—in the drawing program when you create the graphic. That way the process color information gets written into the EPS file and the layout program can recognize it.

STEP 7: TRY COLORS

The original idea was to use two strong colors for the business card, one at full saturation and one screened back. Tsaconas first suggested a lipstick red to appeal to both women and men, but when Ames pointed out that red would turn to pink when it was screened, they both rejected that idea. Ames then worked with a purple and ochre, until she realized that Tsaconas had assumed they needed two colors to get an expensive look. Once Ames explained that they could achieve the same effect with a single color in a solid and a tint, the discussion moved to what that one color should be. Ames had already thought of an Aegean blue, to maintain the Greek theme; Tsaconas independently suggested a teal green. It was clear the two were thinking along the same lines.

STEP 8: COMMUNICATE COLORS

Ames and Tsaconas exchanged ideas by phone, fax and mail. To show her client the colors, Ames sent a printout of the card with a tissue overlay marked with colored pencils. She also included an assortment of Pantone color chips, and Tsaconas picked the final color from them.

The screen doesn't bleed off the stationery and envelope, as it does off the business card (see Production Tip), because it's very difficult to print a bleed on an envelope. In fact, printing a screen on an envelope is difficult anyway, because the flap makes the paper thicker in some places than others, so it's difficult to get even ink coverage. One option is to print the envelope material before the paper is trimmed, folded and glued, but that's only economically feasible in large quantities.

STEP 9: TRANSLATE TO STATIONERY

After the business card was complete, Tsaconas asked Ames to translate the design to stationery. Tsaconas planned to use the stationery not just for letters but also for reports bound into a folder. For that reason, Ames decided to run the design down the side, so it wouldn't look like just a letterhead. The stripe on the stationery had to be narrower than on the business card, so Ames had to break the name onto two lines and adjust the letterspacing. That in turn led to a slight change in the typographic scheme. When the name was on one line, as on the business card, it read as a single element distinct from the "Wardrobes" line. On the letterhead, though, with each word on a separate line, it read as one unit: "Hella Tsaconas Wardrobes." To reestablish the distinction, Ames set "Wardrobes" in upper- and lowercase, a treatment she'll carry over to the business card when it's time to print more of them.

PRODUCTION TIP: The Hella Tsaconas business card is intended to have a 10 percent screen of the teal color covering the entire card—it's set up that way in PageMaker and printed out that way on Ames's laser proofs. However, it turned out that her service bureau's imagesetter was improperly calibrated and printed only a 1 percent screen, which doesn't show up on the final card. The moral of the story: Examine your film carefully, with a densitometer if possible, to make sure you're getting what you asked for.

TRICKY FIGURES

◆ ◆ ◆

Creating a Logo Using a Graphic and Type

Kimberly Fisher doesn't generally do logos, because she thinks you have to know someone well before you can create an identity for them. Friends and family, of course, fall into that category, and happily for Ian Riedel, he qualified as a friend.

Riedel custom-builds bicycles, and he needed a distinctive group of coordinated graphics to mark his product. Fisher agreed to design a logo and several identifying symbols he could use as decals on different parts of his bicycle frames.

Riedel described the kind of image he wanted with a series of adjectives—fun, silly, earthy, wise—and the name of a song: Harry Belafonte's "Day-O." At the time, he was using a hand-drawing of a head in a fool's cap for a logo, and he wanted to keep the jester idea. He also was drawn to American Indian symbols. Finally, he wanted a logo that looked as handmade as his bicycles, not one that was high-tech and polished.

Riedel Cycles Identity
Designer: Kimberly
    Fisher/Fisher & Day
Hardware: Apple
    Macintosh II, Apple
    LaserWriter Plus,
    Abaton 300 GS flatbed
    scanner
Software: Adobe
    Illustrator 88
Font: Futura Extra Bold
    Condensed

SCHELTER & GIESECKE AG., LEIPZIG C1

TAUPERLE

ABCDEFGHIJKLMNOPQRSTUVWXYZ
1234567890

No. 18 616. 8 Pt. 24 A — ¼ Satz etwa 2 kg

SAGEN AUS DEM KLASSISCHEN ALTERTUM

No. 18 617. 10 Pt. 18 A — ¼ Satz etwa 2,2 kg

CODE DE COMMERCE ALLEMAND 3

No. 18 618. 12 Pt. 16 A — ¼ Satz etwa 2,5 kg

ITALIA MERIDIONALE FISICA

No. 18 619. 16 Pt. (Kleine - small - petit - pequeño.) 10 A — ¼ Satz etwa 2,8 kg

BOTANISCHES HANDBUCH

No. 18 620. 16 Pt. (Große - large - grand - grande.) 10 A — ¼ Satz etwa 3,2 kg

NEW OXFORD STREET

No. 18 621. 20 Pt. 8 A — ¼ Satz etwa 3,4 kg

GEWERBEMUSEUM

No. 18 622. 24 Pt. 6 A — ¼ Satz etwa 3,8 kg

HEIMATURLAUB

ZIERDOLMEN

In Verbindung mit Dolmen zweifarbig

No. 18 666. 20 Pt. 16 A — ¼ Satz etwa 4,6 kg

WATERBERG

No. 18 687. 24 Pt. 12 A — ¼ Satz etwa 5,5 kg

ENTREMES

No. 18 688. 28 Pt. 10 A — ¼ Satz etwa 6,3 kg

ILFIORE

No. 18 689. 36 Pt. 8 A — ¼ Satz etwa 10 kg

SAFES

No. 18 690. 48 Pt. 6 A — ¼ Satz etwa 12,6 kg

IMPRENTA

No. 18 691. 60 Pt. 4 A — ¼ Satz etwa 9,6 kg

BREMEN

STEP 1: GET THE FEELING

Fisher started work on the jester figure. With the American Indian theme in mind, she thought of it more as a "trickster" than a medieval jester. She also pictured it as a character composed of geometric shapes but with loose joints, to suggest the calypso flavor of Belafonte's song. Working from this mental image, she started sketching on paper.

STEP 2: CHOOSE TYPEFACE FOR "RIEDEL"

At the same time, Fisher and her partner, Brian Day, started considering different typefaces for a treatment of the word "Riedel" that could stand alone as a logotype and also be turned into a decal for a bike's "down tube" (the part of the frame that runs from the pedals to the handlebars). The face they settled on—a variety of Dolmen called Zierdolmen—came from a book of German typefaces. The blocky letters and in-line design created a pattern suggestive of American Indian designs.

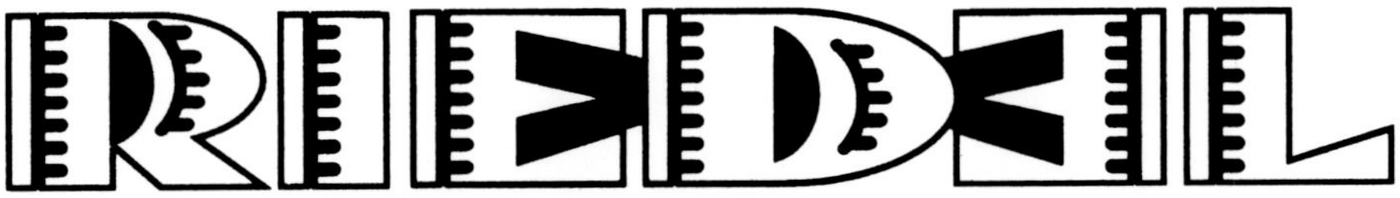

RIEDEL

STEP 3: DRAW "RIEDEL"

Fisher scanned the letters out of the book, traced them in Illustrator, widened them slightly with the Scale tool, and arranged them to spell "RIEDEL." She and Day experimented with different treatments of the letters, one of which flipped the second *E* backwards. When they pinned the result on the wall, they immediately saw the *X* shape created by the interplay of the two *E*s, especially noticeable with the type reversed black-to-white. Fisher liked the effect and decided to go with it for the logotype and decal.

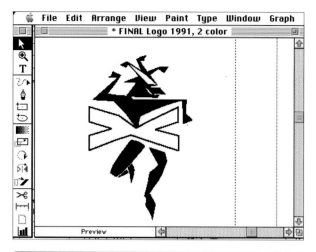

STEP 4: FINISH TRICKSTER

While developing the name treatment, Fisher continued work on the trickster figure. Once she felt she was headed in the right direction, she sat down at the computer to render the figure in Illustrator. She picked up the *X* shape from the "RIEDEL" type treatment and added it to the figure as a sort of skirt. Soon after, the figure was complete.

STEP 6: CONVERT TEXT TO OUTLINES

The now-familiar *X* also suggested a slogan for the builder—*anima x machina*, almost Latin for "life from a machine." To combine the figure with the company name and slogan, Fisher first typed the text, formatted in Futura Bold, and positioned it around the figure. She then converted the characters to individual objects with Illustrator's Create Outlines command so she could color them independently.

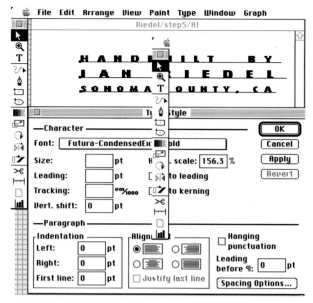

STEP 5: CHOOSE FONT

When Fisher sketches something by hand, she also thinks about what weight and size typeface she wants to use with it. In this case, she had roughed out a simple blocky face that she thought would go with her original trickster figures. Sometimes, she can't find an existing typeface to match her ideas and has to draw one herself, but Futura Extra Bold Condensed fit the bill. The "Handbuilt by" copy appears on a bicycle's chain stay.

When and Why to Convert Text to Objects

Most advanced drawing programs, such as FreeHand and CorelDRAW, now let you convert text to a graphic, as Fisher did for the Riedel logo. When you treat text this way, you end up with a separate object for each letter in the text. Not only can you position the letters exactly as you want them, but you get some advantages during production as well:

◆ You don't have to worry about whether your service bureau has the fonts you used; the graphic is a complete package.

◆ You avoid problems that can arise from printing a graphic with a version of the drawing application or system software that handles fonts differently from your version.

◆ Depending on the program, you may get more flexibility in specifying the type's color if it's converted to outlines first. The main disadvantage is that you can no longer edit the text or change the typeface easily, so try to leave the conversion until the final stages of a project.

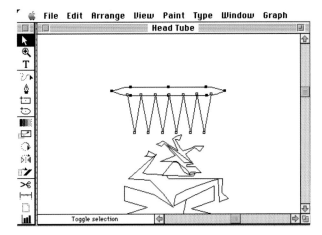

STEP 7: ADD ANCHORING ELEMENTS

With the trickster and the text composed, the logo was almost ready for the head tube (under the handlebars) of a bicycle. Because it would appear to float if placed by itself in the middle of the tube, Fisher surrounded it with graphic elements to visually anchor it. The element over the figure's head is meant to suggest an American Indian–style image of a cloud. It was simply drawn in Illustrator, using the Reflect tool to ensure symmetry.

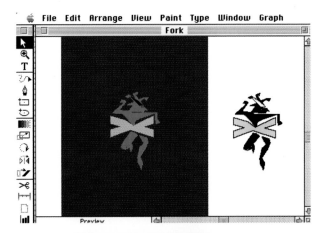

STEP 9: ADD COLOR

Fisher prepared the logos in several different color combinations—black and gold, gray and white, and red and gray—for use on bicycles of various colors. She turned the two-color Illustrator files over to the company that would produce the decals with a special screening process.

STEP 8: EXTEND LOGO

In Riedel's custom-built bikes, the head tube can be anywhere from 2 to 8 inches long, and the decal had to be able to grow to look good at all lengths. To achieve this flexibility, Fisher copied the horizontal element from the cloud above the figure and repeated it in a column below. Riedel can simply cut off as many stripes as necessary to make it fit.

MANAGED COLOR

◆ ◆ ◆

Illustration and Design/Customized Clip Art

Computer Aided Management, Inc. (CAM), manufacturers of the high-end project management program Pariss Enterprise, wanted their new reseller brochure to revitalize the company's image and give it a new direction. CAM gave the Black Point Group partners, Mary Carter and Gary Priester, a fifty-page document describing the company and the product, along with brochures from CAM's competitors. Black Point's assignment was to create something different.

In Priester and Carter's estimation, CAM's competitors' brochures were staid and dull. They decided to go with a relatively "far out" design, relying on a distinctive illustration; vivid, modern colors; and zippy typefaces.

The final brochure can be folded to fit into a #10 envelope, and because it has an open area on one panel for an address, it can also work as a self-mailer. It's a six-color job: the four process colors, a PMS green for the type inside, and a varnish over everything except the business reply card.

Pariss Enterprise Brochure
Designers: Mary Carter & Gary Priester/The Black Point Group
Hardware: 486/33 and 386/33 PC-compatible computers, 14-inch SVGA monitors, Microtek Scan Maker 600Z and Hewlett-Packard ScanJet IIc color scanners, Panasonic and Chinon CD-ROM drives, NEC Silent Writer 2 Model 90 printer.
Software: Aldus PageMaker 4.0, CorelDRAW 3.0
Fonts: Gill Sans, Palatino, ITC Eras Ultra

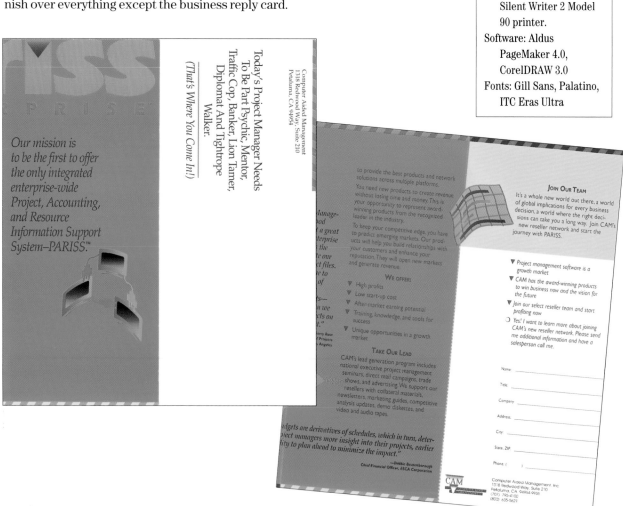

Part I: The Illustrations

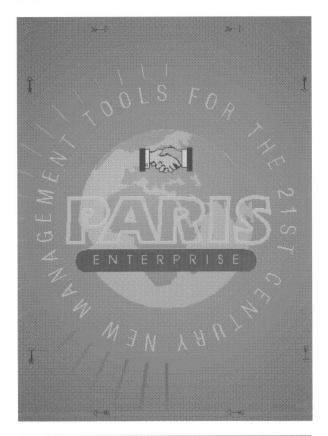

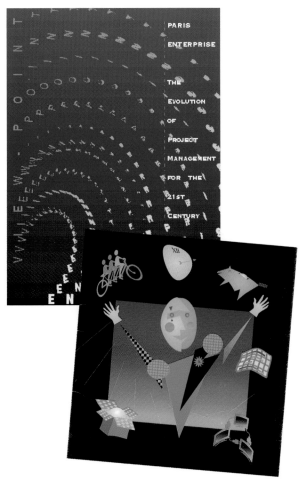

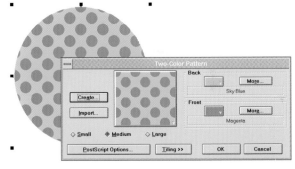

STEP 1: DEVELOP THE ILLUSTRATION CONCEPT

Carter does the artwork for most of Black Point's projects, and Priester does the layout. The two experimented with several different cover concepts, including ones based on the ideas of partnership and evolution, before settling on an approach that illustrated the intended market for the Pariss software. Inspired by a statement in CAM's marketing materials to the effect that a project manager is constantly juggling, Carter created a figure surrounded by air-borne symbols representing (clockwise from upper left) people, time, money, projects, equipment and final product. The *V* shape of the figure's body recalled the company logo.

STEP 2: THE V-MAN'S BODY

Carter assembled the *V*-Man's body out of simple shapes created with Corel's drawing tools. She used the line drawing tool to create triangles for the body and arms and a five-sided polygon for the lapel; the shoulders are circles drawn with the circle tool.

The body and lapel are filled with flat colors, and the left arm is filled with a fountain fill (see the figure for Step 8). The patterns on the *V*-man's "shoulders" and right arm are simple bitmap fills available in Corel. Carter set the size and colors of the dots and checks and then just filled the circle and triangle with them.

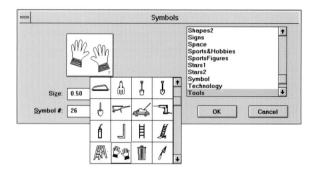

STEP 3: ADD THE HANDS

Carter turned to Corel's extensive clip art libraries for the *V*-man's hands. She chose the Symbol tool from the Text Tool's scrollable pop-up menu and directly imported the image of a pair of gardener's gloves from the Tools library. (In most other drawing programs, she would have had to open the drawing of the gloves and copy and paste them into her working drawing.)

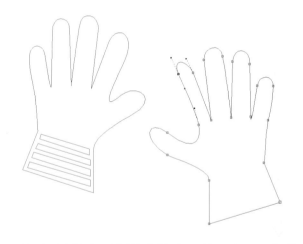

STEP 4: RESHAPE THE HANDS

After importing the gloves, Carter ungrouped them and edited them individually. She removed the stripes on the wrist and thinned and reshaped the fingers to give them more expression.

Working With Clip Art

Designers and illustrators often scoff at the notion of using clip art in their work, feeling that the quality of the drawing is not up to professional standards, or disdaining to rely on someone else's style. They're correct in many instances—much clip art is dreadful, both traditional printed clip art that was intended to be cut out and pasted up, and the electronic clip art that succeeded it. Computer clip art has come a long way, though, and through some judicious selection and editing, you may be able to find or create just what you need.

For her Pariss brochure illustration, Carter incorporated bits and pieces of clip art from CorelDRAW's clip art collections. The computers and plugs below the *V*-man, for instance, come from the library. Often, as here, she'll remove any details from within the drawing and just use it as a silhouette outline.

Carter's approach demonstrates a technique you can use with most currently available clip art. Much of it comes in editable EPS format, which means you can bring it into a drawing program such as Adobe Illustrator or CorelDRAW and rework it: Break it apart, remove parts you don't want, color the pieces as you desire, and rearrange elements. You can also easily find clip art that is more symbolic than pictorial, for use in creating your own signs and generic symbols.

Some electronic clip art produces line art; other clip art produces halftones with texture and detail. The latter is usually sold in TIFF format and is not as easily edited: You can bring it into a paint or image editing program, but you'll need some skill to change it significantly.

Either kind of clip art can be useful, but it's important to pay attention to the style of the artwork. While you can create striking compositions by combining different pieces, it's usually a disaster to mix clip art of different styles.

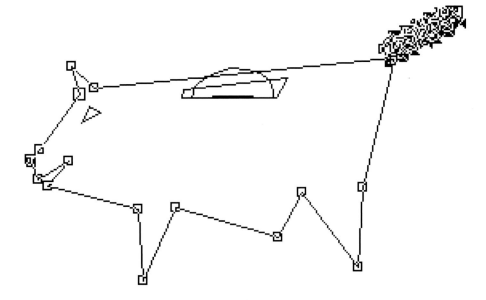

STEP 5: THE FLOWER

The *V*-man's lapel flower
is based on another piece
from Corel's clip art
libraries, from the collection of drawings of plants.
Carter took a flower,
removed the stem and
leaves, and reshaped what
was left. Finally she added
a new triangular center.

STEP 6: DRAW THE PIG

Carter used much the same techniques to create the objects being juggled by the *V*-man;
the pig is a good example of her methods. She drew the outline of the pig with Corel-
DRAW's straight-line tool, simply clicking from point to point to create the basic polygon.
She used the same tool to draw the eye and coin slot, layering them on top of the pig. The
coin was drawn with the ellipse tool and then given the illusion of depth with the Extrude
command. The pigtail came from another of the clip art libraries (it's an electronic circuit
symbol).

Generally Carter draws curves with Corel's freehand drawing tool. This lets her get
close to the shape she wants in a natural fashion, but gives her a line with too many *nodes*
(defining points on the line, called *anchor points* in other programs). After her freehand
sketch, she deletes the nodes she doesn't need and defines the characteristics of the
remaining line segments—whether they're curves or straight lines—to get the figure she
wants.

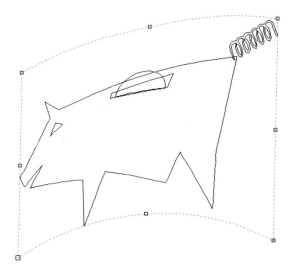

STEP 7: DISTORT THE PIG

After assembling the pig, Carter called on Corel's Edit
Envelope feature to get "handles" around the periphery of
the drawing; by pushing and pulling the handles, she was
able to distort its shape as a whole. She used this feature
on all the little drawings to give them the appearance of
floating on the page.

Both the pig and the coin are filled with a radial fill that
blends between two colors. This is one kind of graduated
fill available in Corel; the other is the linear gradation seen
in the large square in the background and on the *V*-man's
left arm (see the figure for Step 8).

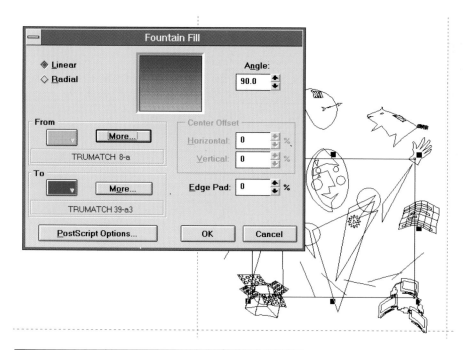

STEP 8: ADD BACKGROUND

To add a background for the *V*-man's juggling action, Carter simply drew a rectangle and filled it with a linear fountain fill (called a gradient fill in some other programs). Then she sent it to the back, behind the various objects.

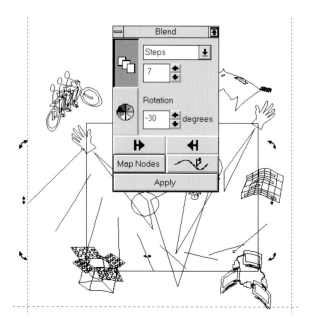

STEP 9: ADD GREEN LINES

The thin green lines sprinkled across the illustration were created with Corel's blend feature. Carter drew a line at one angle, then another line of the same width, length and color in a different place at a different angle. She blended between them in six steps, producing eight evenly spaced lines that rotate across the page. Lastly, she grouped them and used Edit Envelope to distort them further. Carter saved the CorelDRAW graphics as both full-color EPS files and black TIFFs; she entered CMYK values from a Trumatch reference book—which contains samples of carefully printed colors with the CMYK percentages for each—to define the colors in the EPS files.

Part II: The Layout

Priester took over once the illustrations were finished. He added the type on the front panel—above the illustration—in Corel then and saved the entire panel as a single graphic.

Today's Project Manager Needs To Be Part Psychic, Mentor, Traffic Cop, Banker, Lion Tamer, Diplomat And Tightrope Walker.

(That's Where You Come In!)

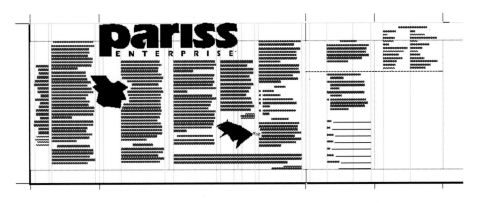

STEP 2: THE LAYOUT

The next step was to start laying out the brochure. Priester imported the black versions of Carter's illustrations to place for position; they would also eventually serve as masks for stripping purposes. Most of the rest of the type on the brochure—and all the small type on the inside—was added in PageMaker, because its type controls are much more extensive and flexible than CorelDRAW 3.0's.

pariss

pariss

pariss

ENTERPRISE ™

STEP 3: CREATING "PARISS"

The word "Pariss" was typed in CorelDRAW in Erie Black, Corel's version of ITC Eras Ultra. The diamond over the *i* was drawn separately and filled with a blend. Then the whole graphic was saved as both a black TIFF and a color EPS file. Priester brought the black version into PageMaker to use as a general placeholder; since the word would extend across a cut in the brochure, he left the final positioning up to the printer.

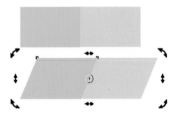

STEP 4: CREATE A COMPONENT OF BORDER

Priester added a "railroad" border to the brochure as a decorative element that adds unity to the piece and repeats the strong colors used throughout. To create the border, he started by drawing a rectangle in CorelDRAW. He copied it, pasted in the copy, and placed the two rectangles side by side (the two together are 1½ inches wide). Then he gave them each a different color fill. Finally he skewed the pair 15 degrees forward.

STEP 5: REPEAT THE COMPONENT

To turn the pair of skewed rectangles into a strip for the border, Priester selected and moved them, specifying a horizontal offset of 1½ inches— exactly the width of the rectangles. Turning the Leave Original option caused the two lozenges to be duplicated during the move. He repeated the command (Control-R in Corel) until he had eleven pairs. Finally, he selected all the pairs, grouped them, and scaled the group to the proper length for the panel. He saved a color version and a black version for import into PageMaker.

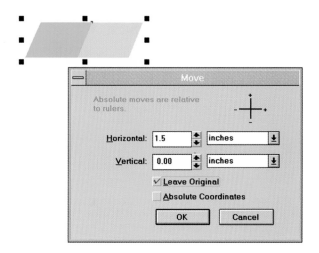

STEP 6: SEPARATIONS AND PRODUCTION

Priester placed the color versions of his railroad border in the same file as the color EPS versions of Carter's illustrations. He sent the whole group as an EPS file to Black Point's service bureau for separation. At the same time, he had the PageMaker file run out as a black-and-white mechanical. The four-color film from the EPS separations was stripped into the film made from the PageMaker mechanical. The placed black versions of the graphics showed the stripper where they went, and the stripper was able to use traditional means to choke the background a little to avoid trapping problems. The body type was printed in a special green PMS color. That color, and the solid colors for the background, were called out in instructions to the printer on the mechanical.

COLORFUL PARTY

◆ ◆ ◆

Digital Design and Layout With Die-Cuts

When Jane Rainwater was ready to dedicate her new studio, she decided to mark the event—which was also the tenth anniversary of her design business—with a reception for friends and business associates. Her first impulse was to base the invitation on some reproductions of her past projects, but after roughing out a few concepts, she abandoned that idea in favor of something bolder (and less expensive).

Rainwater started to play with the idea of hands, as a symbol of her handiwork and as a way to count off ten years. She turned to a favorite pair of red polka-dot vintage gloves and started working with the idea of incorporating a visual of them into her design. She also decided she wanted the invitation to be somehow three-dimensional.

She created a simple, elegant, but striking three-panel folded invitation. For added interest, she had the invitation die-cut so parts of it would pop out when opened.

*Rainwater Design
Invitation*
Designer: Jane Rainwater/
    Rainwater Design
Hardware: Apple
    Macintosh II, Apple
    LaserWriter Plus,
    Microtek 600ZS
    scanner
Software: Aldus
    PageMaker, Aldus
    FreeHand, Adobe
    Photoshop
Fonts: Futura Extra Bold
    Condensed, Palatino

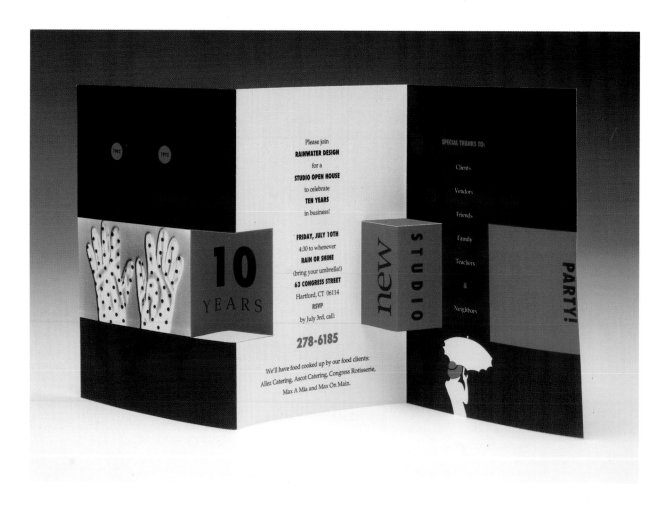

STEP 1: THE LAYOUT

Working from a thumbnail she'd sketched on the back of a message pad, Rainwater started to draw up the design in PageMaker. She started with a three-panel design that would fit in a #10 envelope, but switched to a more distinctive A-6 size. The color breaks were determined from experiments with markers on black-and-white laser printed comps.

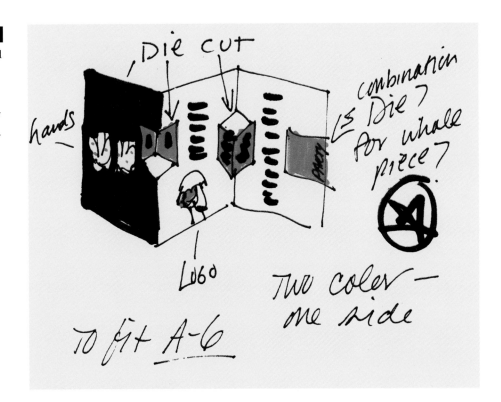

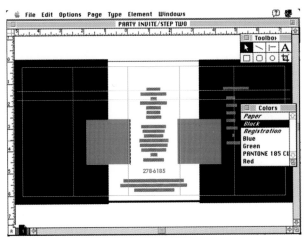

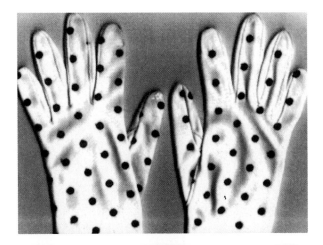

STEP 2: THE GLOVES

To get a picture of her gloves, she simply put them directly on her scanner and scanned them into Photoshop as a gray-scale image. She experimented with different treatments—adjusting the brightness and contrast, changing the entire background to black, inverting the gloves so that they were white dots on black, and so on. In the end, though, she settled on something that looked pretty much like the original gray-scale scan, with only minor touch-up.

STEP 3: ADD THE LOGO

The figure with umbrella had been Rainwater's logo long before she owned a computer. When she started working electronically, she digitized the logo with FreeHand by tracing the figure onto acetate, taping the acetate to her monitor, and then drawing behind it with FreeHand's Curve tool. That was before she owned a scanner, of course; now she would simply scan the logo and use the scan as a template. For this project, she created two versions, one in color for positioning in the PageMaker file, and one in black and white that the printer used to make film for stripping into the final page films.

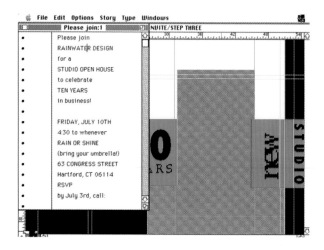

STEP 4: ADD TEXT

Rainwater typed all the copy in PageMaker, using the program's Story Editor. This word-processor–like module allowed her to type in the text, then place it in the proper location.

Please join

RAINWATER DESIGN

for a

STUDIO OPEN HOUSE

to celebrate

TEN YEARS

in business!

FRIDAY, JULY 10TH

4:30 to whenever

RAIN OR SHINE

(bring your umbrella!)

63 CONGRESS STREET

Hartford, CT 06114

RSVP

by July 3rd, call:

278-6185

We'll have food cooked up by our food clients:

Allez Catering, Ascot Catering, Congress Rotisserie,

Max A Mia and Max On Main.

STEP 5: FORMAT TYPE

While still in the Story Editor, she formatted the text with the proper typefaces—Palatino, her longtime corporate typeface, which she chose for its gentle appearance; and Futura Extra Bold Condensed—the chunky nature of this sans serif made a nice contrast with Palatino. The sideways type was turned with PageMaker's Text Rotation feature.

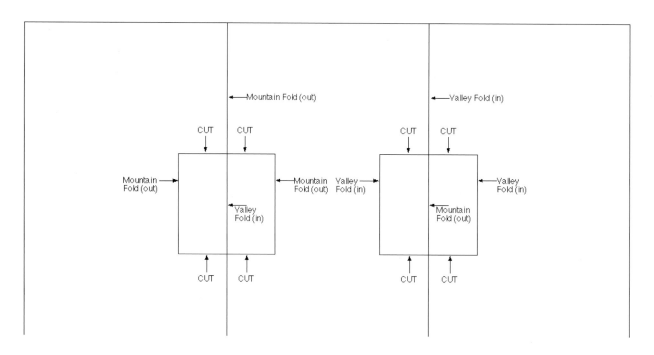

STEP 6: PREPARE DIAGRAM FOR DIE-CUTTER

The first production step was to create a detailed diagram for the die-cuts. She drew the diagram in FreeHand and gave it, on disk, to the die-cutter so he could start setting up the cutting machinery properly. She also saved a simplified version as an EPS file, imported it into PageMaker, and fine-tuned her layout to make sure it conformed accurately to the die.

The Importance of a Good Printer

Jane Rainwater credits the success of her invitation to the quality of the printer she works with. The piece uses a simple design that depends on solid, even ink coverage. Without a good printing job, the piece would have looked drab; gaps or "hickies" in the color would have diluted the impact of the design's geometric blocks and vertical type.

The printer also had to take care of trapping in areas like the two little red dots and the "Special Thanks To:" red-on-black line, so that there wouldn't be any paper showing through. Again, imagine a white gap around either of those elements, and you can see that the design would have been ruined.

You can address some of these problems yourself (for instance, by creating your own traps), but some problems you can't control, no matter how expert you become with your computer and design programs. The moral: Don't underestimate the effect of traditional skills—or skimp on their use—when doing electronic design.

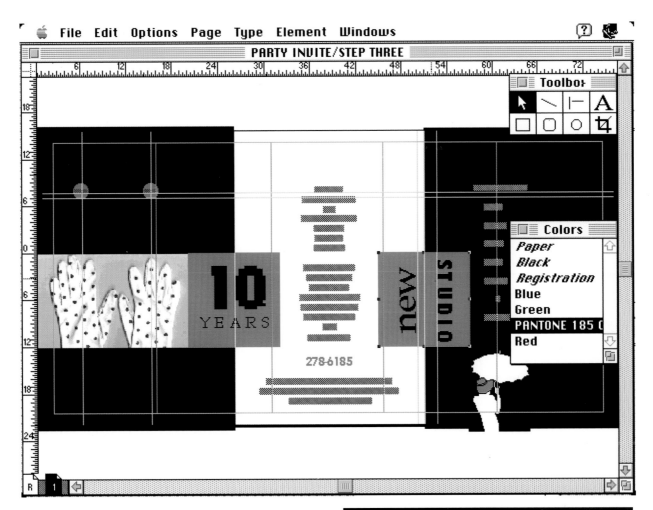

STEP 7: SEPARATIONS

Rainwater left the trapping up to her printer, since her version of PageMaker didn't really offer a way to handle trapping. She did make spot color separations—separate plates for the red and black elements. Working from Rainwater's color comp of the design showing color breaks and PMS specifications, the printer used traditional techniques to trap the separations.

SEASON'S GREETINGS

◆ ◆ ◆

Illustrations Plus Photo Manipulation Equals Pizazz

I t's pretty much *de rigueur* for a design studio to create its own holiday cards. TechArt, one of the first electronic design firms in San Francisco, didn't shrink from the challenge. For their 1991-92 Season's Greetings effort, the TechArt staff wanted to come up with something colorful and fun that would also identify the staff members by name.

They decided to base the card on a staff photograph, colorizing it and adding a couple of special effects. They surrounded the photo with symbols of holiday cheer and an appropriate message to produce a warm, amusing greeting to send to their friends, customers and associates.

TechArt 1991-1992 Holiday Card
Designers: Susan Equitz & Denise Lever/TechArt San Francisco
Hardware: Apple Macintosh IIcx, Hewlett-Packard ScanJet Plus, Linotype L-300 Linotronic Imagesetter, Apple LaserWriter NTX
Software: Adobe Photoshop 2.0, Adobe Illustrator 3.1, QuarkXPress
Fonts: Futura Condensed Extra Bold, Copperplate 33BC

STEP 1: SCAN PHOTOGRAPH

The designers started with a black-and-white staff photo-graph that had been taken for another use. First, they scanned it as a gray-scale TIFF. To add color, they took the duotone feature of Adobe Photoshop in an unusual direction. Duotones are usually printed with a black or dark gray for the shadow tones and a lighter gray or muted color for the highlights. TechArt decided to stay with a dark/light contrast but to look for bolder colors.

STEP 2: CHOOSE COLORS

The designers wanted colors that offered a contrast in both brightness and hue but would blend well in the photo nonetheless. After some experimentation in Photoshop, they settled on a dark purple (PMS 2593) for the shadows and a warm green (PMS 5773) for the highlights. The combination gave the faces a yellowish tone, similar to an old sepia photo.

Care With Color Names

When working with more than one program, it's a good idea to make sure that your colors retain the same name throughout your project. Even with standard color reference systems, you need to be careful. For instance, even though both Illustrator and Photoshop are made by Adobe, they don't call their Pantone colors by exactly the same name—Pantone 5773 CVC in Photoshop 2.0 is Pantone 5773 CV in Illustrator 3.1. That could cause problems if you bring something from each program into another program for separation, as TechArt did with its holiday card. The final program may not recognize that the colors are the same and will consequently put them on different plates.

For this reason, TechArt was careful to make all their color names uniform, down to capitalization and spacing. Furthermore, since at first they didn't plan to create any green objects in QuarkXPress, they were careful to at least define the green color in that program. Otherwise, XPress wouldn't have known the color existed, and wouldn't have properly separated any of the imported green objects. As it turned out, they used a tint of the green color anyway, for the embossed photo on the back of the card.

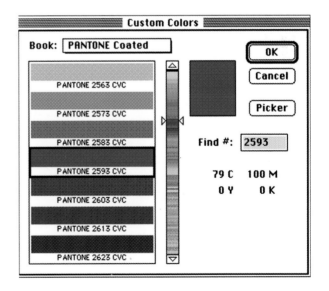

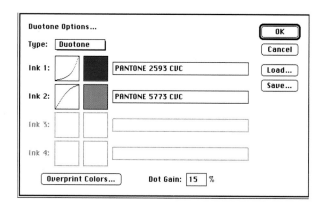

STEP 3: CREATE
DUOTONE

The designers brought the
scanned photo into Photo-
shop as a gray-scale image
and selected Duotone
mode. That brought up the
Duotone Define Colors
dialog box, into which
they entered the names of
the two Pantone colors
they had chosen (Pantone
5773 CVC and Pantone
2593 CVC).

Don't Get Caught in a Trap!

Many of the projects described in this book bring up the problem of trapping. *Trapping* is the generic term for a variety of techniques that compensate for the possibility of bad registration when you print multiple colors. For example, in the TechArt Christmas card, the green "From All of Us at TechArt" text would ordinarily *knock out* the purple background; in other words, no purple ink should be printed where there is green, and vice versa. (If you just printed the green over the purple, green would change in appearance where it overlays the purple ink.)

The problem arises because, while two colors may butt against each other perfectly on your screen, you can't be sure your printer can keep the two colors registered—that is, lined up perfect-ly with each other. If one shifts a little bit, you'd see a gap of white paper in between the two colors. That's where trapping comes in.

Trapping basically means expanding (*spreading*) the foreground or shrinking (*choking*) the background slightly so that the two colors overlap enough to cover any potential gap. You can leave trapping to your printer, whose time-tested methods involve masking one color and slightly enlarg-ing the resulting hole when making the film. Since this is so much a part of the services a printer traditionally provides, it's difficult to say just how much of your printing bill it might account for, but, as in most areas, doing it yourself may save you some money. Plus, if you supply film rather than a mechanical, you *must* take care of trapping yourself.

The most common approach to trapping on the desktop is the one taken by the staff at TechArt, which is to use a drawing program's stroking feature to place a thin line around the foreground object. Set the line to overprint, and it will print on top of the background and should cover any gap. QuarkXPress offers an automatic trapping function for colored objects created within the pro-gram, and some XTensions help deal with trapping imported objects. Finally, some high-end color separation systems can read a PostScript page file, turn the whole thing into a giant bitmap, and trap the file based on the colors in the bitmap.

You can also avoid the problem of gaps altogether. If you place a black or white rule around objects as part of your design, for instance, the rule will serve the function of an overprinted stroke. Another technique is to make sure the foreground and background colors have a color component in common. This doesn't work where the colors are special inks, as in the two-color TechArt job (each color is a separate PMS ink), but works for four-color separations.

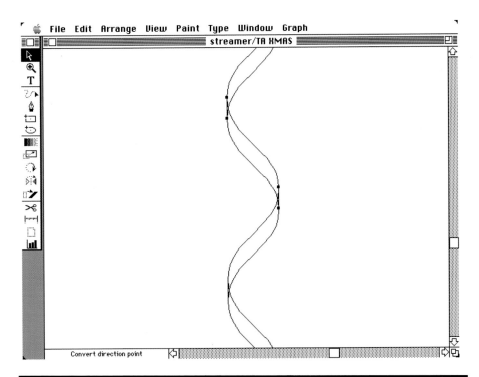

Convert direction point

STEP 4: CREATE STREAMERS

The designers turned to Illustrator to create the streamers; each one is a repeated series of two curved shapes, one shaded light and one dark to suggest the front and back of a ribbon. They started with a simple *S*-curve, duplicating and moving it slightly and closing the ends to make an open *S* shape. Then they reflected the shape vertically to make the alternate shape.

To shade the segments, they turned the open shape into a mask with Illustrator's Paint command. Then they created the illusion of graduated fills by creating two objects with different fills and blending between them. By placing the *S* shape behind the blend and grouping them, the shape "punches out" part of the blend, making it appear as though the *S* has a graduated fill. For the dark side of the ribbon, the blend goes from 50 percent in the center to 100 percent at the ends; for the light side, it's 20 percent in the center and 70 percent at the ends. Finally, they strung together series of the two-part segments to make each streamer.

STEP 5: STRETCH STREAMERS

Because all the streamer segments were identical, and the streamers looked unnaturally regular, the designers simulated the way a thrown ribbon would stretch by first selecting all the segments except the last one and increasing their length to 103 percent; then, they selected all but the last two, increased the rest, and so on. The sections were also rotated slightly to make the streamers curve gently.

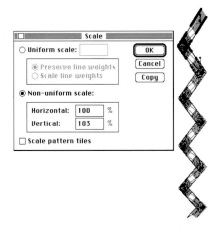

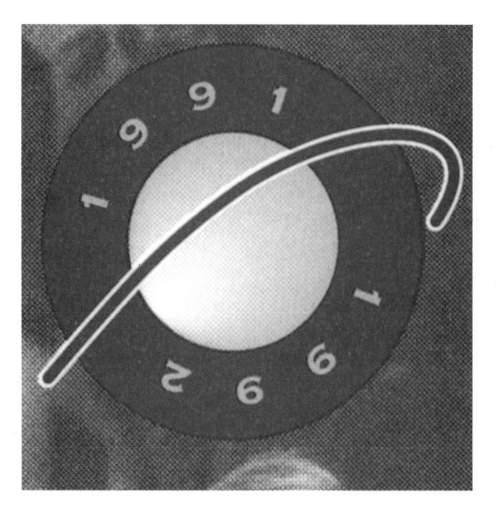

STEP 6: CREATE GLOBE

The globe of the 1991-1992 planet "bug" was built out of two circles—a large circle filled with a 90 percent screen of the green color, and a tiny circle in the lower left of the larger one filled with a 5 percent screen. Blending between the two created the spherical effect. The type "1991" and "1992" was set on a line a little larger than the globe. Finally, a purple circle was placed behind the globe and a "ring" drawn around it. The ring is composed of one white line about 2 points wide, with a 1-point purple line on top of it, both with rounded end caps.

STEP 7: CREATE BORDER

The entire border of the picture, type included, was created in Illustrator. The "From All of Us" line is set in Futura Condensed Extra Bold and rotated 90 degrees. The "Season's Greetings" line is set in Copperplate and extended to the proper length with Illustrator's Tracking command at a setting of 460/1000 ems.

TechArt handled the issue of trapping here, as elsewhere in the Illustrator file, by overprinting a very thin green stroke around any green object. On the "From All of Us" text, for instance, the type is filled with 100 percent green—which knocks out the purple color behind it—and outlined with a .5-point 100 percent green stroke, which overprints the purple. The overprinted green stroke covers any misregistration between the type and the background.

After assembling the photo, border, streamers and other elements in XPress, the TechArt designers still needed some way to identify the individuals on the staff. They hit on the idea of reprinting the photo, flopped, on the back of the card. First they considered a screened-back halftone, as though the paper were translucent. But they finally decided that using an embossed version would make it easier to read the identifying signatures. So they used Photoshop's Emboss filter at its default settings, saved the result as a grayscale TIFF, and applied the green color in XPress.

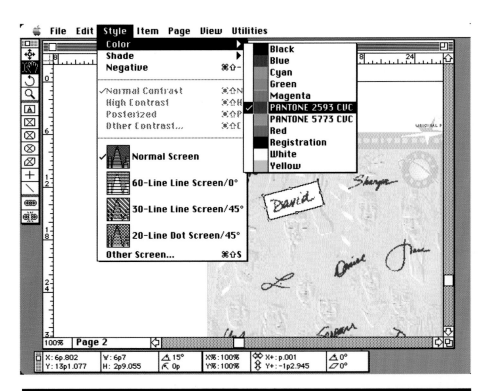

The signatures were scanned off regular paper as 300 dpi black-and-white bitmap files. They were imported into graphics boxes in XPress and colored there.

ARTISTIC VISION

♦ ♦ ♦

Package Graphics

Revo makes high-quality, expensive sunglasses. The company always spent a lot of money on research and development, but never much on promotion. During the 1980s, however, the sunglasses market changed, becoming more competitive and more reliant on product image. When Revo approached Nason, the company was burdened by inconsistent packaging that didn't represent the quality of the product line.

Nason decided to focus her efforts on the glasses themselves—to make the sunglasses the "hero of the story" rather than models or lifestyles. Since Revo's technology is based on blocking the part of the light spectrum that causes hazy and blurred vision, Nason decided to create an image to suggest light shining through the glasses, with the long shadow staying sharp all the way to the end.

*Revo Sunglasses Package
and Collateral*
Designer: Lori Barra
    Nason/TonBo designs
Hardware: Apple
    Macintosh IIci, Apple
    LaserWriter IINT,
    Apple Scanner
Software: Aldus
    PageMaker 4.2, Adobe
    Illustrator, Applescan
    scanning software

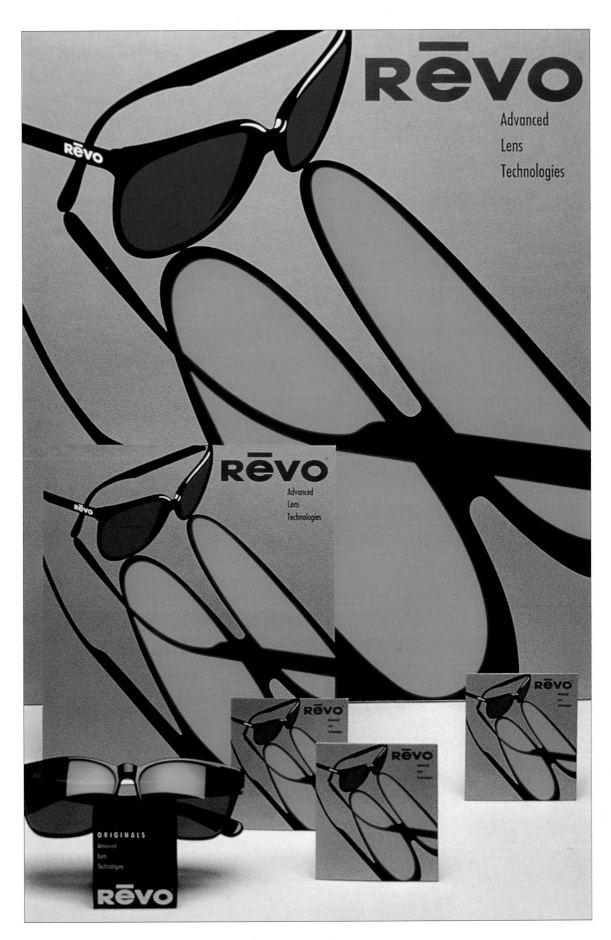

STEP 1: SCAN PHOTO

The first project was to be a poster, and Nason decided to base it on a "mood piece" photo. She lit a pair of the sunglasses in such a way that they'd throw long shadows, and shot it to make a very crisp image. But after mocking up some boxes with the photo, she realized that it wasn't going to be as versatile an image as a graphic, and wouldn't work for applications where four-color printing wasn't available, such as T-shirts and embroidered caps. So she decided to turn the photo into a graphic that would work in two or three colors.

The first step was to scan the photo of the glasses and shadow as line art to get a very high-contrast image. She saved the scan as a MacPaint bitmap file.

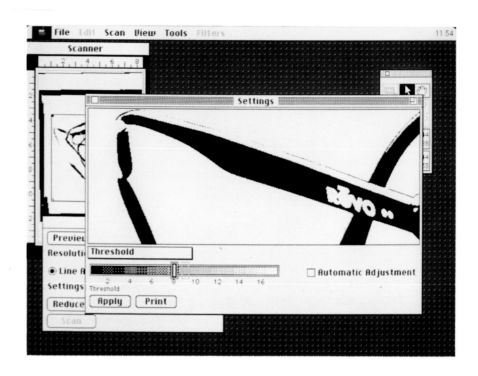

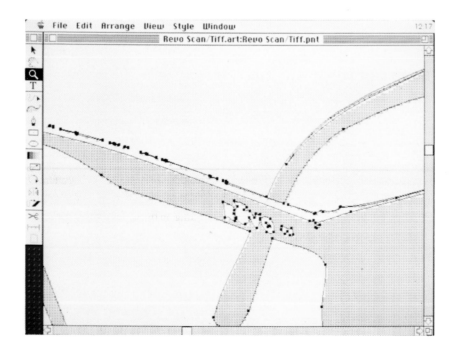

STEP 2: AUTOTRACE SCAN

After opening the Mac-Paint scan as a template in Illustrator (shown in gray), Nason used Illustrator's automatic tracing function to get a working outline of the glasses.

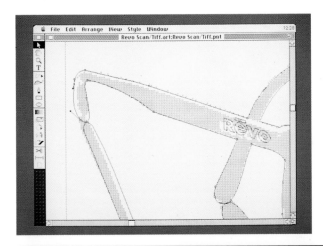

Automatic tracing is often better used as a starting point than as a final image, because by following every tiny curve and flaw in the template art, it can produce a graphic with more points than you need. After autotracing, Nason used Illustrator's drawing tools to clean up the outlines, deleting points where necessary.

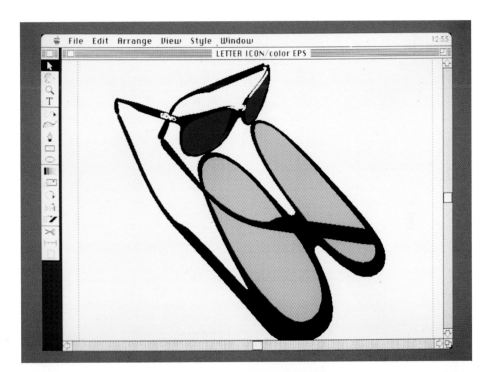

STEP 4: ADD COLOR

The sunglasses drawing came out as several closed paths that could be treated as separate objects. Nason filled them with various colors, depending on the style of glasses involved. She used the colored versions to print comps of the graphic for her clients.

STEP 5: REDO LOGO

Nason also modernized and strengthened the company's treatment of its name. The outline version of the logo on the new package is similar to Revo's original logo since the company wanted to retain the established identity. Nason scanned the old logo and traced it in Illustrator. She then used Illustrator's tools to reshape and balance the letters, making them chunkier and more solid. In addition to the outline version, she saved a filled version that holds up better at small sizes and can be more easily imprinted on the glasses themselves than the outline version.

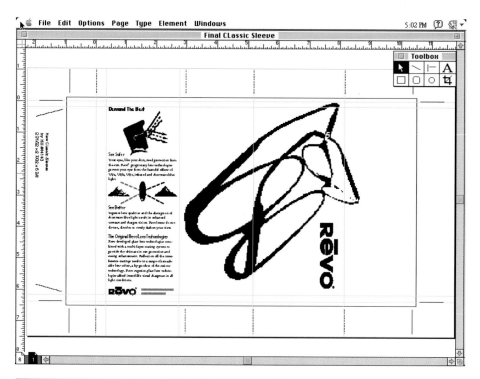

STEP 6: MAKE PACKAGE MECHANICAL

The final packaging was to be produced from black-and-white mechanicals, with the color added at the printer. Nason brought the black-and-white version of the sunglasses into PageMaker, where she had set up a page to match the shape of the box outline. She arranged the sunglasses—and the Revo logo—in their proper positions. All the areas that would print in color were outlined or surrounded by black, so Nason instructed the printer to print all the black parts of the mechanical as black, and on a tissue overlay she indicated which other colors were to print where. The printer was able to use the black mechanical as a mask and handle trapping himself.

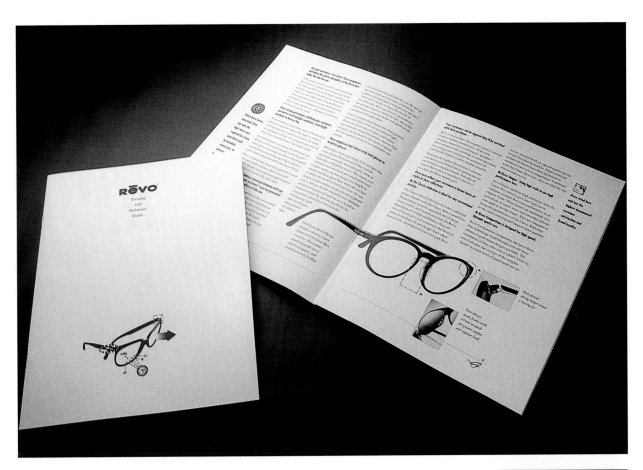

STEP 7: ADAPT TO TRADEMARK

Revo also uses a "Training and Reference Guide" to instruct shop owners on how to display and market the sunglasses properly. For the cover of the guide, Nason used the same glasses, but with the shadows removed and symbolic graphics added. That treatment of the glasses became the company's trademark, used on its letterhead and stationery. The image was also easily adapted to other purposes, such as a poster and in-counter display system.

UNCONVENTIONAL INSURANCE
• • •
Recycled Art From Annual Report to Ad

Centre Reinsurance, one of the world's largest professional reinsurance companies (it insures other insurance companies), basically does one promotional effort per year— its annual report. Since it's a once-a-year effort, the company puts a lot into it and needs to get a lot out of it. WYD Design, which has produced the company's report for the past several years, tries to make the piece as striking and memorable as possible.

The designers also leverage the annual report for Centre Reinsurance's ad campaign. The ad, which plays off the annual report, appears in trade publications amidst a lot of conservative insurance ads. WYD's concept goes a long way toward positioning Centre Reinsurance as an innovator in the field.

"I LOOKED AND, BE[

What happens when a 3-D stranger visits a two-dimensional world? Call us at 800-295-8501 to receive a complimentary copy of our 1991 annual report, "Beyond Flatland: New Dimensions in Reinsurance."

Admittedly, Centre Re is not like most reinsurers. Nor is our approach to solving insurance related problems. But, in growing numbers, companies are opening their eyes to the benefits of finite risk products. And they're startled by the possibilities.

MORE THAN MEETS THE EYE. The concept of finite risk may not be new, but m[applications are. Flexible finite risk products are being used by more companies a[problem-solving tools for hard-to-manage risks and extraordinary losses. They p[stability, loss financing and risk transfer necessary for reinsurance, while solving m[complex problems the traditional market is unwilling or unable to accept.

LD, A NEW WORLD"

SEEING IS BELIEVING. Since 1988, Centre Re has written more than $2 billion in finite risk products to meet a wide variety of insurance and reinsurance challenges——from catastrophes to corporate restructuring. For more information about how we can help you reach your risk management and financial goals, contact us or your insurance or reinsurance intermediary.

CENTRE RE

INNOVATION IN REINSURANCE
MEMBER OF THE ZURICH INSURANCE GROUP

Rated AA by Standard & Poor's

*Centre Reinsurance
   Advertisement*
Designer: WYD Design
Hardware: Apple
   Macintosh IIci,
   SuperMac 19-inch
   color monitor, Howtek
   ScanMaster color scan-
   ner, QMS ColorScript
   color thermal printer
Software: Aldus
   PageMaker, Adobe
   Photoshop, Adobe
   Illustrator
Fonts: Bodega Sans
   Oldstyle, Metropolis
   Shaded, Phyllis,
   Belucian

STEP 1: RESCAN ART

The large piece of art-work, a three-dimensional assemblage of objects, was created by Henrik Drescher, photographed as a 4x5 transparency, and scanned for use in the annual report by WYD's printer on his Scitex system. WYD had several extra copies of the printed version of the artwork made for their own use, and vice president Randy Smith scanned one of those copies for use in the ad layout. Since the image had already been half-toned for printing, Smith had to turn it slightly on the scanner bed to eliminate any moiré patterns.

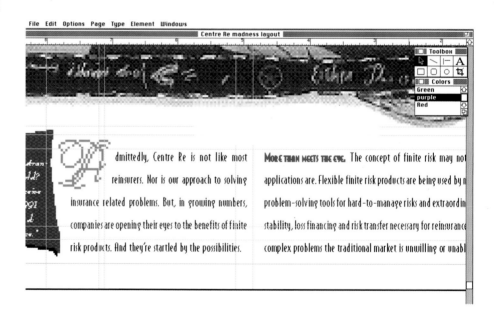

STEP 2: FORMAT TEXT

Smith arranged the text—written by WYD vice president Frank Oswald—in PageMaker and started experimenting with different typefaces. He ended up with Bodega Sans Black Oldstyle for the headline and Bodega Sans Oldstyle for the main text face. It's a sophisti-cated but quirky face, and fits with the style created for the annual report. The *A* is set in Phyllis.

STEP 3: IMPORT LOGO

The Center Re logo is an Adobe Illustrator graphic, previously created by WYD. Smith imported it into PageMaker as an EPS file.

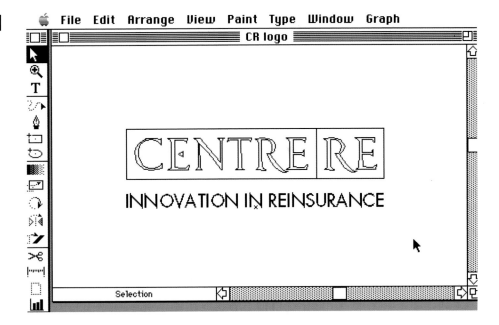

STEP 4: IMPORT SCRAP OF ART

The swatch of purple in the corner was also created in Illustrator. It was drawn to look like a scrap of color that came from the main piece of art. After it was drawn, it was duplicated, filled with black, and offset to give it a shadow. The text was placed over it in PageMaker.

Smith sent his Page-Maker file of the ad to WYD's printer, who read it into his Scitex system through a Dolev Post-Script interpreter and separated it with the Scitex tools. The printer stripped the separated photograph into the page film by traditional means.

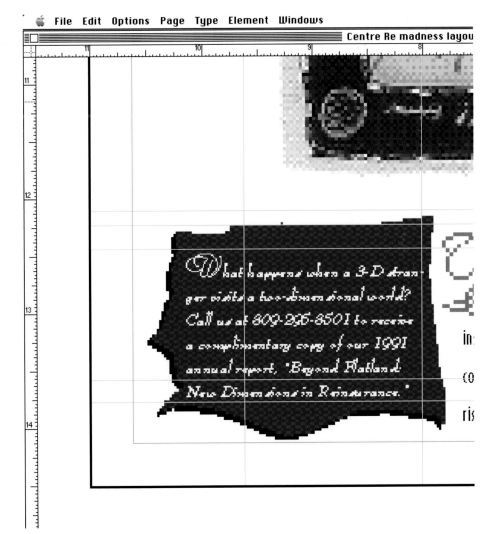

BOLD EXPRESSIONS

• • •

Enhancing Ordinary Photos With a Photo-Editing Program

Jerry Wagers wanted to wrap his first venture as a solo musician in a cassette cover that would reflect the intimate, romantic mood of his music. Designer Johnathon Caponi and art director Sharon Anderson chose portraits from existing Polaroids to reflect this mood. They decided to use close-up photographs of the artist, made slightly mysterious by being screened into the background. They further decided that the unpretentious look and rough-hewn texture of stencil letters would give the cover the right finishing touch.

The most challenging aspect of the job was the tight budget. To keep costs down, Caponi used Polaroid photos and laid out the cover in three panels instead of the usual five. This meant that he had to fit all the lyrics into a small area and still keep them legible.

Jerry Wagers Cassette Cover
Art Director: Sharon Anderson
Designer: Johnathon Caponi
Hardware: Apple Macintosh IIci; Agfa Focus Color Plus Flatbed scanner; Agfa Selectset 5000 imagesetter; Linotronic imagesetter
Software: Adobe Photoshop, Adobe Illustrator, Adobe Separator
Fonts: Helvetica Neue Heavy Extended, DIN Newzeit Grotesk Bold Condensed

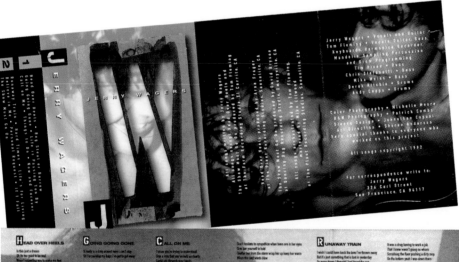

STEP 1: SCAN PHOTOS

Caponi started by scanning the three Polaroid photos of Wagers on the Agfa Color Plus flatbed scanner, using the Agfa scanning module for Adobe Photoshop. He set the scanning resolution to 300 pixels-per-inch (ppi) and the scaling to 200 percent, giving final scans double the size of the original photos with 150 ppi resolution.

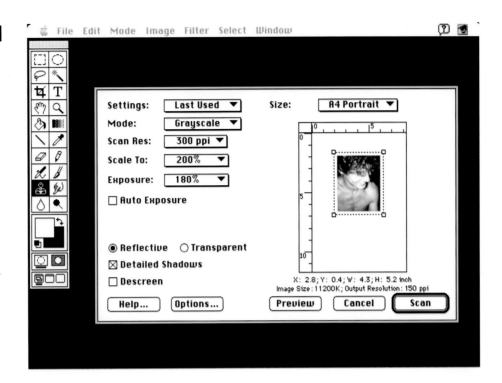

STEP 2: LIGHTEN IMAGE

After scanning the photos, he used Photoshop to match them to the originals with the Levels and Brightness/Contrast commands. Then he applied the Equalize feature to make the darkest areas gray and lend a photocopied effect. Finally he used Brightness/Contrast again to wash out some of the details in the highlights of the face.

The next step was to lighten the image overall so it would be in the background on the cover. Caponi selected the entire portrait and filled it with white, set to an opacity of 35 percent. That whitened all the pixels without changing the tonal balance.

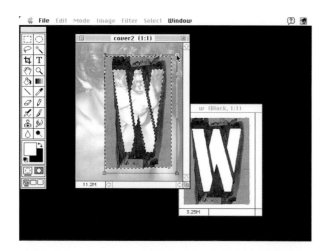

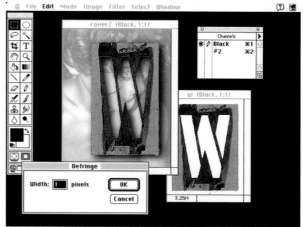

STEP 3: ADD THE "W"

The *W* (and the *J* initial cap on Wagers's name) were scanned from a cardboard stencil. Caponi isolated the *W* from its white background by using Photoshop's magic wand tool to automatically select all the white and then chose Inverse to select just the stencil. Next, he copied and pasted the *W* onto the Wagers photo. Because the stenciled image was a little smaller than the portrait, he lengthened it with Photoshop's Scale command.

STEP 4: ADD SHADOW

Caponi next copied the *W* to the clipboard and opened a new "alpha" channel to add a shadow to it. In the new channel he chose Offset from the Filters menu and moved the selection 15 pixels right and 15 pixels down, repeating the edge pixels. Next he applied a Gaussian Blur, specifying a radius of 10 pixels, to soften the shadow edges.

Caponi returned to the black, or main channel of the portrait image, loaded the shadow, and filled it with 100 percent black. Then he chose Paste to position the original stencil back on top and into position. Finally he chose Defringe, specifying one pixel, to smooth the stencil.

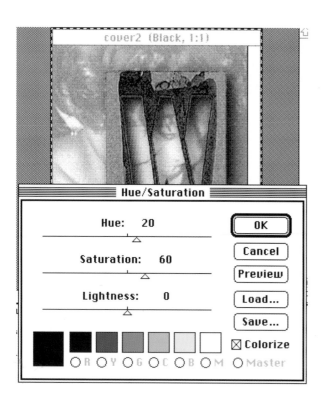

STEP 5: COLORIZE STENCIL

The next step was to colorize the gray-scale image. Caponi converted the image to RGB mode and chose Hue and Saturation from the Image/Adjust menu. After clicking on the Colorize checkbox, he adjusted the Hue slider to match the original color of the stencil, then brought the Saturation slider down to make the color less intense.

STEP 6: CREATE BASE FOLDOUT IMAGE

For the dual-image foldout, Caponi wanted to create an image approximately 5.5" x 4.5", with a resolution of about 266 ppi. In Photoshop, he started by rotating the close-up of Wagers 90 degrees counterclockwise. Then he chose Image Size and set the resolution to 266 ppi. Since the original scan was 150 ppi, increasing the resolution this way made the image smaller. It was still larger than he needed, though, so he returned to Image Size, unchecking the Constrain File Size checkbox to prevent resampling, and set the height to 4.5 inches; the width changed in the same proportion, ending up slightly smaller than 5.5 inches. To remedy this, Caponi

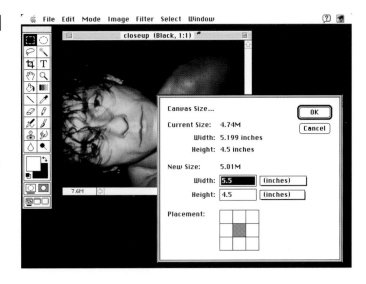

selected Canvas Size and set the image width to 5.5 inches. The extra canvas was filled with black, the background color.

For the second image to the right of the close-up, he repeated these steps with another scanned photo, but without rotating or inverting it. This gave him two canvases of the same size, each with a different photo.

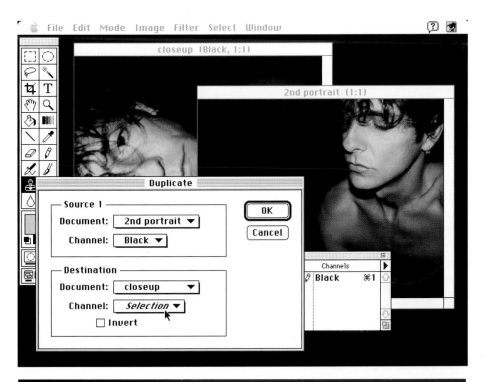

STEP 7: ADD SECOND IMAGE

Since both image sizes were the same, Caponi chose Duplicate from the Image/Calculate menu. He specified the second (unrotated) image as the source and the Selection channel of the first (close-up) photo as the destination, and filled the duplicate with 35 percent black. Both the cover image and the foldout panel images were then converted to CMYK mode and saved as EPS files for import into Illustrator.

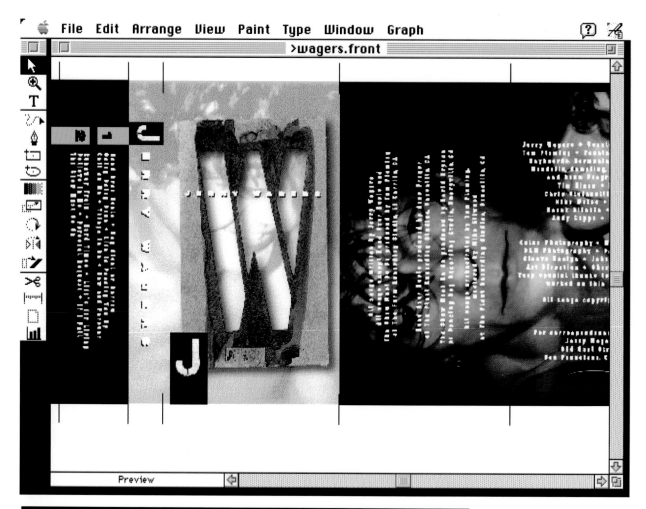

STEP 8: ASSEMBLE THE IMAGES

Caponi assembled the images and set the type in Adobe Illustrator. After creating a template of the dimensions for each panel—as specified by the printer for a three-panel cassette cover—he placed the cover and foldout images in the Illustrator file and moved them into their correct positions. He set the credits and song titles in DIN Newzeit Grotesk Bold Condensed because of its legibility at small sizes and its compact and modern look.

DYNAMIC COMPUTER DESIGN

70

STEP 9: ADD FINAL TOUCHES

Since the cover image was light, Caponi gave the white "Jerry Wagers" title—set in Helvetica Neue Heavy Extended—a black shadow. He had the shadow overprint the cover image to avoid any trapping problems.

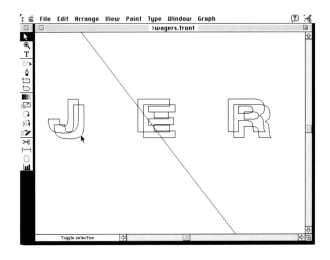

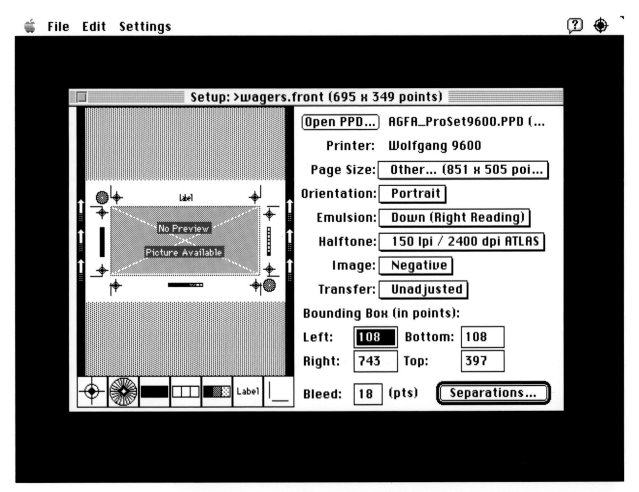

STEP 10: PROOFS AND SEPARATIONS

The final file was proofed as a gray-scale file from Illustrator on a Linotronic imagesetter at high resolution. Once approved, Caponi saved the Illustrator file in EPS format. Finally, he used Adobe Separator—which comes with Illustrator—to separate the file to film on an Agfa Selectset 5000 imagesetter.

FOR ART'S SAKE

• • •

Adding Special Art and Text Effects

When David Salanitro was head designer for the Fresno (California) Art Museum, he worked on everything from exhibit planning to the museum's identity package. During that period, the museum had also expanded both its physical space and its exhibit selection. By the time Salanitro moved away from Fresno, the museum had improved in many areas, adding events and performances to its mix of attractions.

The museum's newsletter, though, hadn't kept up with the changes. It still had a bare-bones layout, and the people who received it didn't keep it—they threw it away and then called the museum to find out what was going on. Salanitro offered to redo the newsletter and, based on his mockup of a sample cover and interior page devoted to events listings, the museum accepted his offer. Besides giving the newsletter a more lively appearance, Salanitro presented an idea for the events page that included an article about the museum's activities to encourage a sense of community between the museum and the newsletter readers.

Preview, *the Newsletter of the Fresno Art Museum*

Designer: David Salanitro/ David Salanitro Studio

Hardware: Apple Macintosh Quadra 700, Radius 19-inch color monitor with Radius 24-bit display card, Microtek 300Z grayscale scanner, LaserWriter II

Software: QuarkXPress 3.1, Adobe Photoshop 2.0, Aldus FreeHand 3.1

Fonts: Palatino, Janson Text, Akzidenz Grotesk, Berthold Script, Emigré Journal

Q. **What to do with time on your hands?** (answer inside)

in this issue: bugs and beetles

PREVIEW

winter 1992

STEP 1: COVER HANDS

Salanitro started by taking two Polaroid photos—one of a stopwatch and one of a person holding his head. He scanned them both as gray-scale TIFF images.

The watch as scanned wasn't as big as the person's face, so Salanitro's first step was to remove the head—otherwise, the face would be visible above and below the watch. He simply used Photoshop's lasso tool to select the head, and with the background color set to black, he pressed Delete, replacing the head with a solid black field.

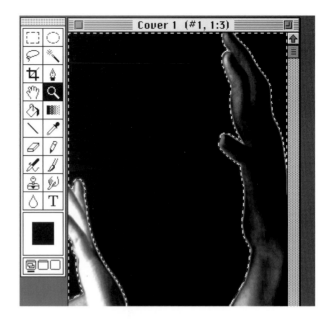

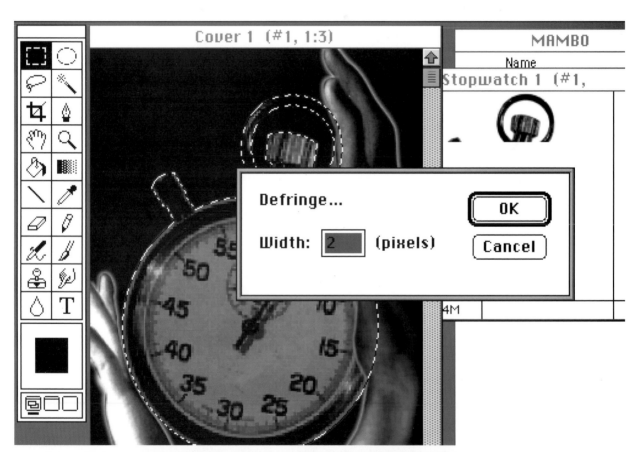

STEP 2: PASTE WATCH

Salanitro opened the scan of the watch and copied the stopwatch. He then returned to the picture of the hands and selected the left hand. Choosing Paste Behind caused the watch to be placed so that the left hand was superimposed on it. With the watch still selected, he moved it into the proper position. Finally, he selected Defringe, with a setting of 2 pixels, to blend in the edge of the watch.

STEP 3: RESIZE IMAGE

The composite image wasn't the size or shape Salanitro needed for his layout. He made it fit by entering the proper values into the Image Size dialog box, after unchecking Constrain Proportions. That also gave the image an interesting elongated effect.

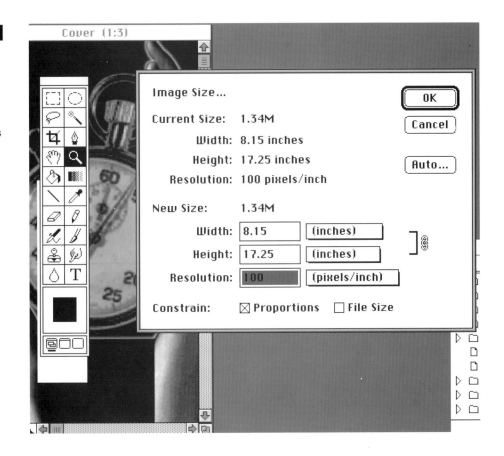

STEP 4: ADD NOISE

Salanitro saw two possible problems with the ultimate reproduction of his image. One was that to get a halftone at the size he'd scaled the photo to, he would have to scan the images at such a high resolution that the file size would be huge. The other was that the newsletter would be printed on inexpensive paper, so the photo wouldn't reproduce well anyway. He decided to exploit the low resolution as a design element and used Photoshop's Noise filter to emphasize the graininess of the image.

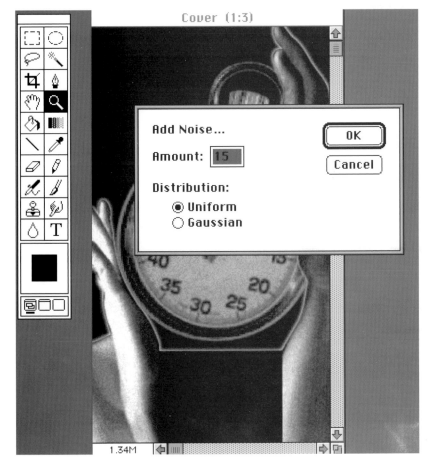

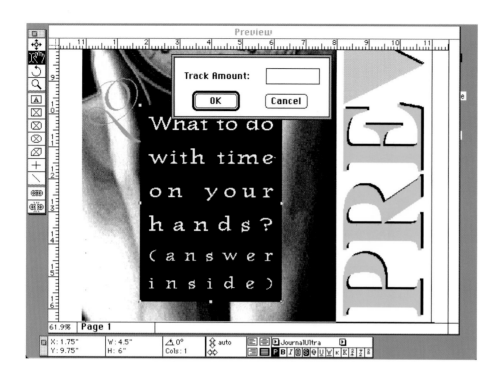

The "What to Do" copy on the cover is in an XPress text box with the copy set in the arty, informal Emigré Journal typeface. To justify the text, Salanitro selected each portion of text he wanted to fall on a separate line and adjusted its tracking to widen or shrink the space between the letters until the lines broke as he wanted.

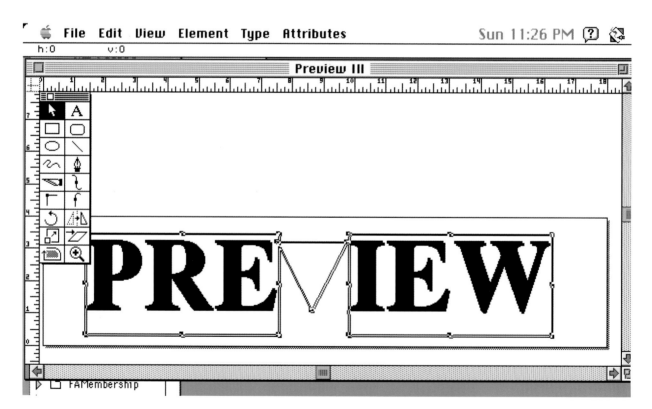

STEP 6: CREATE NAMEPLATE

Salanitro created the "Preview" nameplate in FreeHand. First he typed in the letters, leaving a space for the *V*. He then converted the letters to paths and modified them somewhat, to change the shape of the letters and adjust the letterspacing. Then he drew a triangle in place of the *V* and filled it with gray. He grouped the entire word, duplicated it, and offset the duplicate in order to create a drop shadow. After rotating the nameplate, he saved it for import into XPress.

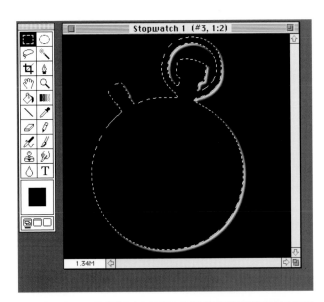

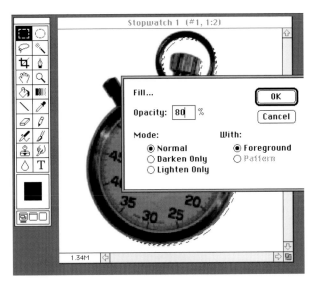

STEP 7: CREATE DROP SHADOW

Salanitro picked up the stopwatch from the cover and used it on the interior page, along with some coins. He wanted to add dimension to the image of the stopwatch by giving it a shadow. First he selected the stopwatch and made a mask out of it, using Photoshop's Save Selection command. Doing it again gave him three channels: the original image and two identical masks. He shifted the second mask with the Offset filter and gave it a 2-pixel Gaussian Blur to fuzz the edge. Then he loaded the first mask into the second mask's channel and subtracted it from the second mask, leaving a blurry crescent shape.

STEP 8: IMPORT SHADOW

After the shadow's shape was completed, Salanitro brought the composite, crescent-shaped mask into the original image's channel and filled it with 80 percent gray. The result is a shadow that fades convincingly toward the edges.

STEP 9: ADD COINS

Salanitro created the coin images by placing the coins directly on the scanner bed. The hourglass-shaped shadow, which gives the coins a believable shiny appearance, was an unexpected benefit of doing it this way.

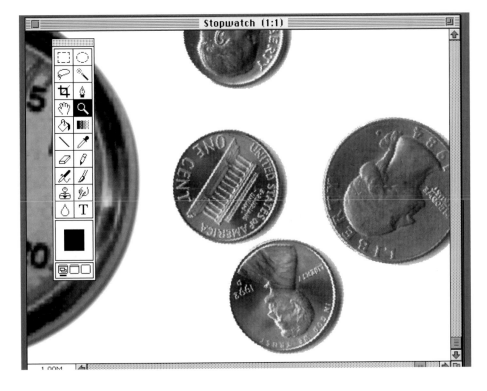

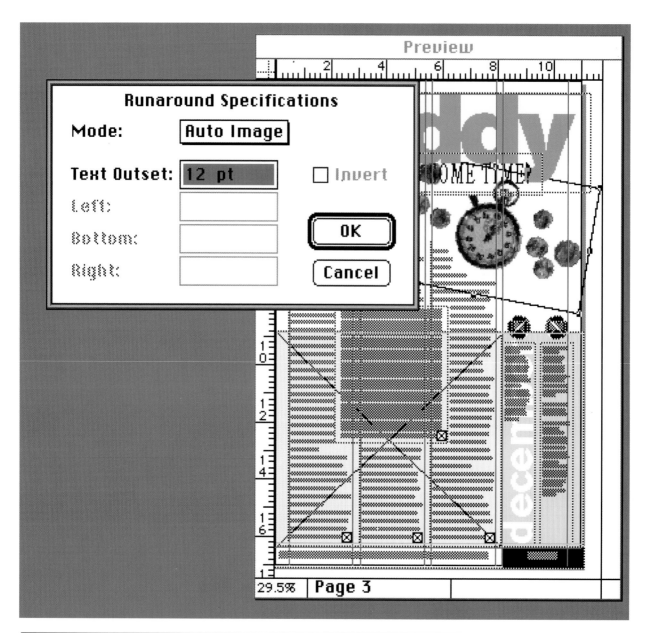

STEP 10: ADD TEXT TO THE EVENTS LISTING

The text on the interior page is formatted in three separate text boxes, linked so the copy flows from one to the next, with the drop cap *C* sitting in yet another text box. Salanitro set the Runaround command for the drop cap's text box to Item so the copy would follow the borders of the text box. On the other hand, he set the Runaround on the graphics box holding the watch to Auto Image, so the copy would follow the contours of the watch itself rather than its box.

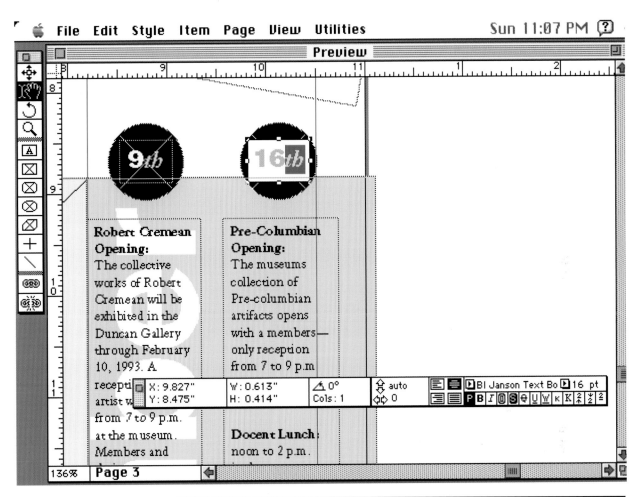

STEP 11: FORMAT CALENDAR LISTING

The calendar listing is made up of four layers of XPress boxes. At the bottom is a text box filled with the orange background color and the word "December" in white, rotated 90 degrees. On top of that is another text box with no background color and black type, for the events listing. Next are two circular picture boxes with black backgrounds and on top of them, centered manually, are transparent text boxes containing the words "9th" and "16th."

The museum newsletter uses only two colors: the orange (a PMS shade, done in various tints and screens) and black. The files were printed as spot color separations, on two pieces of film.

FAST FOOD, FAST PACKAGING

◆ ◆ ◆

High-Speed Computer-Based Design

In October 1992 Jones Dairy Farm approached Design North about a package design for their new convenience breakfast food—a sausage wrapped in a pancake. The problem was, Jones needed the packages completed by the following January, when the product was to be introduced. Worse, the company needed complete mock-ups of the packages by the first week of November, when the TV ads were to be shot.

Jones specified two requirements the package design had to meet. One was that it clearly distinguish the three flavors the product came in; the other was that it show the product so the consumer could quickly tell what it was.

The one thing the designers had to start with was the product name—"Jiffies," thought up by Jones's advertising agency, Frankenberry, Laughlin, and Constable. By relying on an extensive in-house computer publishing setup, Design North was able to make the deadline.

Jones Dairy Farm "Jiffies" Package
Designer: Design North, Inc.
Hardware: Macintosh IIfx, Barco Calibrator 19-inch color monitor, RasterOps 24L graphics card, Sharp JX600 scanner, Optronics ColorGetter scanner, Optronics Colorsetter 2000 imagesetter, QMS ColorScript Model 100 color printer
Software: Aldus FreeHand, QuarkXPress, Adobe Photoshop, Prepress Technologies SpectrePrint Pro
Font: ITC Stone Serif

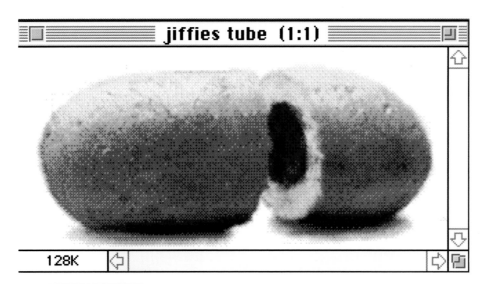

jiffies tube (1:1)

128K

Jones Dairy Farm supplied Design North with actual samples for the product shots. The designers took several photos of each product—some on a plate, some with ingredients nearby, some whole, some cut—to provide a variety of choices for the final layout. The photos were scanned at low resolution with the Sharp JX600 and brought into Photoshop to remove the background.

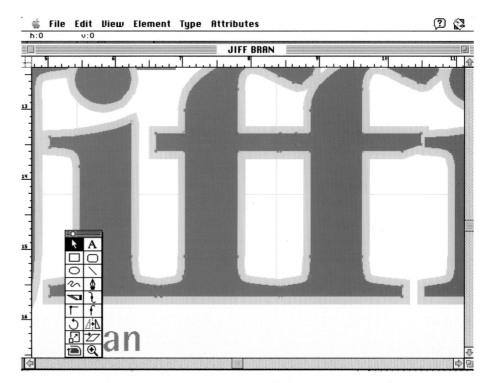

File Edit View Element Type Attributes

h:0   v:0

JIFF BRAN

STEP 2: DESIGN PRODUCT NAME

Design North wanted to make the product name a recognizable symbol as well as just a word, so they went beyond a simple type treatment, turning to FreeHand to manipulate the type. They started by setting the word "Jiffies" in the distinctive ITC Stone Serif, then kerning the letters until some of the serifs (on the bottoms of the *f*'s, for instance) were touching. Next they converted the letters to paths for further manipulation. Since each letter was now a separate object, they were able to move them around even more and modify their outlines slightly. These alterations helped make the word a distinctive trademark while keeping it legible.

Color Proofing Devices

You can design in color on screen, but to get a good idea of what your document will look like, you need to see it on paper. There are several different color proofing devices to choose from:

◆ Thermal wax transfer printers—These are probably the most common color printers in use as proofing devices. Such printers use a heated print head to melt tiny dots of colored wax from a roll of film onto the paper. The printer uses the process colors—cyan, magenta, yellow and sometimes black—and overlays halftone screens to create different colors, just as in four-color printing. The resolution on these proofs is only 300 dpi, however, so halftones are coarse. These printers work well for proofing documents with flat color and text, but not so well for photos.

◆ Inkjet and bubblejet printers—These are the least expensive color printers. They spray liquid colored ink onto the paper, and most have their own *dithering* patterns for mixing different colors. The results are often a smoother blend than you can get from a thermal-transfer printer, but the inks generally provide less vivid color than the wax does.

◆ Dye sublimation printers—These printers also use heat to apply color to the paper, but instead of melting wax, they *sublimate* dyes from film. The dyes are transparent, so the colors—again, cyan, magenta, yellow, and in most cases black—can be overlaid on each other. The color is laid down in tiny tiles that butt against each other, giving complete paper coverage and a photographic appearance. That makes these printers good for proofing continuous-tone images; their relatively low resolution makes them less suited for proofing text.

◆ Digital color printers—These are extremely high-end inkjet printers that produce photographic-quality proofs. They're far more expensive than the other kinds of printers, though.

Other proofing methods are based on the actual separated film; these methods have been around for a long time. Brand names for this kind of proof include Cromalin from DuPont and MatchPrint from 3M, both "integral proofs" that produce one piece of paper; and Color Keys from 3M, which consists of four layers of film laid over a white sheet. The advantage to these proofs is that, since they're made from final film, they're a better representation of what you'll get on press than proofs made from a digital file.

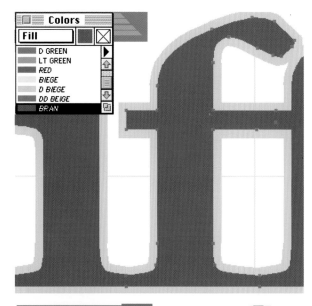

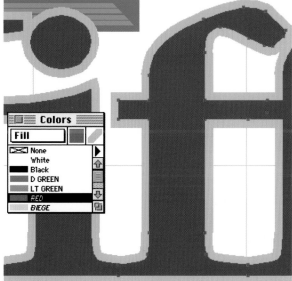

STEP 3: COLOR THE LETTERS

Each flavor variety features the word "Jiffies" in a different color. All the colors were first defined in FreeHand as process colors so they'd appear in each file's color palette, and then they were applied to the letters. Achieving the effect of one outline around several touching letters took some trickery, since the letters were separate objects: If the designers had simply used the Fill and Stroke commands on each letter, the outlines would have overlapped. Instead, each logo is made up of two layers: The bottom one has a red fill (the color for the buttermilk flavor) and a gold stroke, and the top one has a fill of whatever color goes with that flavor (purple for the Multi Grain, for instance) and no stroke. The effect is of a purple (or blue, or red) letter with a gold outline.

STEP 4: ADD JONES'S LOGO

Jones Dairy Farm supplied its logo as original art, and the designers rendered it with Adobe Illustrator, specifying the proper Pantone colors. FreeHand can both open and place Illustrator EPS files, so it was a simple matter to add the logo, colors and all, to the file with the "Jiffies" name.

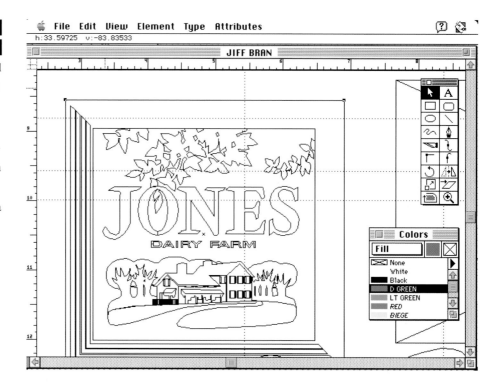

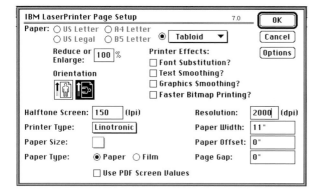

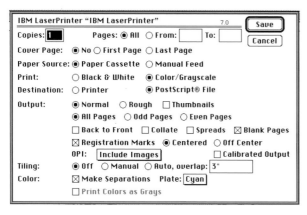

STEP 5: MAKE SEPARATIONS

Most of the front panel of the box was designed in Free-Hand, but the designers turned to XPress for final assembly and separations. When the time came to actually produce the packages, the designers scanned the product photos again on the high-resolution ColorGetter. They color-separated the photos with SpectrePrint Pro, saving them as Desktop Color Separation files (see box). Then they replaced the original Sharp scans of the product shots in XPress with the new high-resolution scans. Finally they brought in the front-panel EPS file from FreeHand and arranged it properly.

To separate the file, they printed one PostScript file at a time from XPress to disk—one for each color plate. Then they sent those files to the Colorsetter with a downloading utility.

Design North prepared DuPont Cromalin proofs from the separated film. Cromalins use dyes to create a positive color proof on heavy paper (like a photographic print). The Cromalins were scored and folded into full-color, high-resolution mock-ups of the boxes and served as stand-ins for the real boxes in Jones's television commercials.

•BRAN KEY 11/29

STEP 6: DESIGN BACK PANEL

The back-of-the-box material was added last—it wasn't visible in the commercial, so it didn't have to show on the stand-in boxes. Most of the material is text, and Design North simply composed and rotated it in Quark-XPress. The happy child was drawn in FreeHand by one of the designers and imported into XPress.

Desktop Color Separations

One of the more elusive goals of desktop publishing systems has always been truly push-button color separations of pages containing photographs and other continuous-tone art. (Finding a program to separate just the photos themselves is comparatively easy.) One of the more successful approaches, yielding accurate, high-quality color, is to use Desktop Color Separation (DCS, also called EPS5) files.

To create DCS files of a scanned photo, you would generally use a program with separation capabilities—usually an image-editing program, such as Photoshop or PhotoStyler, or separation software, such as SpectrePrint Pro—to convert the scan to a CMYK image. Then, after making any desired color corrections or other changes, you save the file in EPS format, choosing the Desktop Color Separation (or whatever your program calls it) option. The program generates five separate EPS files (hence the EPS5 name): one each for the cyan, magenta, yellow, and black layers, plus a separate "composite" file linked to the other four.

You then place the composite file into your layout program that can print separations. When you print, the program automatically replaces the composite file with the correct separated file for each color plate. The separated files can contain all the color and halftone information you set up in the image-editing program (or you can leave the halftoning to the layout program).

Besides the overall awkwardness of the process, the main drawback to this technique is that the five EPS files take up a lot of disk space—each file, by itself, can easily be double the size of the original scan file. But it's still the best desktop method, since it assigns the task of separations to the software best suited for it—an image-editing or separation program.

DELUXE TREATMENT
◆ ◆ ◆
High-End Design and Production

It's called an Annual Report on the cover, but while it contains some financial information, it's really more of a capabilities brochure. RELO is an association of real estate brokers specializing in housing for relocated executives. Because RELO's clients are the corporations who pay the relocation expenses, the report is designed to appeal to corporate tastes. The images, materials and techniques throughout are luxurious—marble patterns, vellum flyleaves, and photos of expensive accommodations. Five colors are used for the printing: the four process colors and a fifth match color. A textured cover with gold embossing wraps up the package.

*RELO Corporation
Promotional Brochure*
Designer: Pamela C. Rice/
P/R Design Group, Inc.
Hardware: Apple
Macintosh IIsi's,
Magnavox and NEC
Multisync 15-inch color
monitors, GCC and PLI
removable hard disk
drives, UMAX 600 dpi
color flatbed scanner,
Datacopy gray-scale
flatbed scanner,
Hewlett-Packard
LaserJet IIP with
PostScript cartridge
Software: Letraset
ImageStudio, Adobe
Photoshop, Aldus
FreeHand, Adobe
Illustrator,
QuarkXPress
Font: ITC Fenice

THE INTERNATIONAL RELOCATION NETWORK

ANNUAL REPORT

RELO®
THE INTERNATIONAL
RELOCATION NETWORK

The era of the multinational business community is well under way. With it comes increased demand for cost-effective employee relocation services to support corporate needs both here and abroad.

1991: A BENCHMARK YEAR IN CORPORATE RELOCATION

The year was marked by turbulent political and social change. It began ominously with military conflict in the Mideast. It ended with democratic reform sweeping across Europe and the former U.S.S.R.

While the media focused its attention on these and other world events, commerce continued. However, it was clearly not 'business as usual.' Indeed, 1991 was a year of dramatic economic transition, especially in the real estate sector.

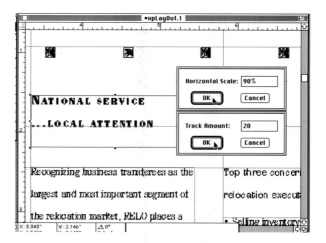

STEP 2: FORMAT HEADINGS

For the headings, Rice chose ITC Fenice Ultra. She used XPress's Horizontal Scaling feature to condense the face to 90 percent of its standard width, emphasizing its verticality. To keep the condensed type from looking too crowded, she increased the tracking to 20 with XPress's Tracking feature. That kept the headings' apparent weight in line with the widely leaded text.

STEP 1: CHOOSE TYPEFACE

Rice wanted a distinctive typeface for the brochure, something conservative but with some flair. She chose ITC Fenice because she liked its tall, thin appearance and the balance between thick and thin strokes.

STEP 3: CREATE DROP CAPS

QuarkXPress has an automatic drop-cap feature, but it doesn't allow the text to wrap to the shape of the letter. To get the body copy to flow around the *R*, Rice typed the letter into a separate text box and positioned it in the corner, specifying a runaround of None. Then she drew an empty picture box roughly the shape of the *R* with the polygon tool and placed it over the drop cap. With the wrap on the picture box set to Manual Image, she had a manipulable border she could use to control the text wrap.

STEP 4: ACQUIRE PHOTOS

The photographs in the brochure were supplied by the RELO members. Rice had the largest images scanned on a service bureau's slide scanner; she used her color flatbed scanner to scan prints of the smaller slides. (The prints were made on a Vivitar slide printer.) She used the scans as For Position Only images to work out her design, then had the photos separated traditionally and stripped in.

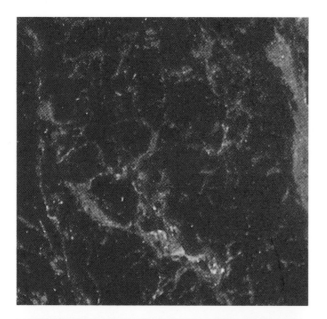

STEP 5: CREATE MARBLE TEXTURE

The marble textures used as accents throughout the brochure come from scans. When working out the initial design, Rice scanned a sheet of paper that had a marble texture on it and saved the scan as a TIFF file for import into XPress. She printed that version on her comps; for the final brochure, she substituted a high-quality scan of a 4x5 transparency of a piece of marble.

SCANNING TIP: Look for objects with interesting patterns that you can scan and drop into your documents for spot art or backgrounds (see "Captured Images," page 9). Try lace and fabrics, or get samples of countertop materials from a home supply store and scan them. Paper, of course, comes in all sorts of patterns, ranging from pebbles to polka dots.

You can also scan three-dimensional objects, if you're careful. Try pressed flowers, or even leaves and pine needles. For these last, though, it's a good idea to arrange them on a piece of white cardboard and wrap it well with plastic wrap or sandwich them between two pieces of glass to keep dirt and dust out of your scanner.

STEP 6: ADD TRIANGLE

Rice used XPress's polygon tool, which lets you make a picture box of any straight-sided shape, to create the triangle at the top of page 2. She then imported her marble scan and specified the color as a CMYK combination, with an 80 percent screen applied to tone down the color intensity. The additional marble shapes were created with XPress's other picture box tools.

Working With Color in QuarkXPress

QuarkXPress allows you to specify colors by a variety of methods: Hue, Saturation and Brightness, which correspond to the way color is described in color solids; Red, Green and Blue, the three colors used on a color computer screen; Cyan, Magenta, Yellow and Black (CMYK), the process colors; or the Pantone, Trumatch, or other color specification system. No matter which system you use to define a color, you can select Make Separations, which separates any color created in the program into its CMYK components—no matter how you specified the color—or, alternatively, print it on its own sheet as a spot color.

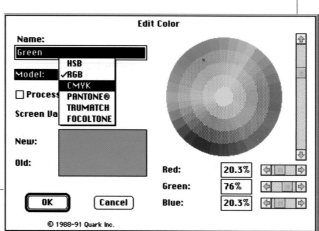

Charts From a Drawing Program

For years, graphic artists have been using drawing programs to produce charts and graphs, because their type, layout and color capabilities so far exceed those available in spreadsheet and other charting programs. You can save some effort by using a graphing program to create bars (or wedges of a pie chart) of the proper size and then bringing the graph into a drawing program for refinement. There are several ways to do this:

◆ print the chart and scan it for use as a template for tracing, as Rice did;

◆ take a black-and-white screen shot of the chart on screen and load that into the drawing program as a template;

◆ copy the graph to the Clipboard and try pasting it into the drawing program; this doesn't work with Illustrator, but with MacDraw you get an image you can ungroup and edit.

Starting with version 3.0, Adobe Illustrator includes a charting module with which you can create column, pie, and other standard types of graphs and later edit them like any other drawing. The drawback is that if you ungroup the chart to modify its appearance, its connection to the data is lost. Illustrator's direct selection tool lets you work on the chart without ungrouping it, though.

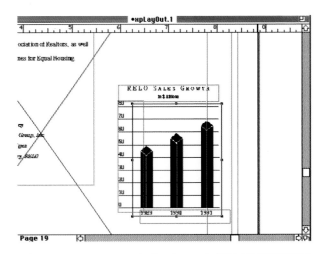

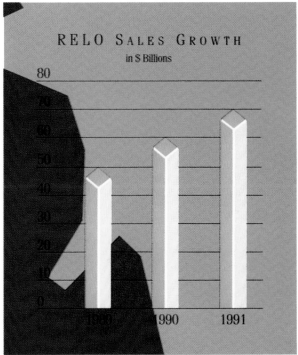

STEP 7: THE BAR GRAPH

Rice began work on the chart by entering the data into Microsoft Excel, a spreadsheet program with built-in graphing abilities. She then printed the graph and scanned the printout to use as a template in Illustrator. After tracing the template and saving the result in EPS format, she brought the chart into FreeHand to work out the colors. She prefers the tracing tools in Illustrator but feels Free-Hand is better for color work. She saved the colored chart as an EPS file and imported it into XPress. Finally, the labels were added in XPress, in text boxes overlaying the chart.

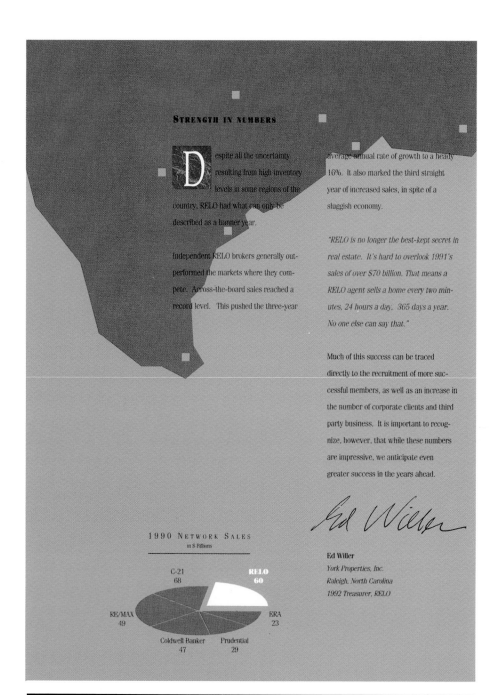

STRENGTH IN NUMBERS

Despite all the uncertainty resulting from high inventory levels in some regions of the country, RELO had what can only be described as a banner year.

Independent RELO brokers generally outperformed the markets where they compete. Across-the-board sales reached a record level. This pushed the three-year average annual rate of growth to a heady 16%. It also marked the third straight year of increased sales, in spite of a sluggish economy.

"RELO is no longer the best-kept secret in real estate. It's hard to overlook 1991's sales of over $70 billion. That means a RELO agent sells a home every two minutes, 24 hours a day, 365 days a year. No one else can say that."

Much of this success can be traced directly to the recruitment of more successful members, as well as an increase in the number of corporate clients and third party business. It is important to recognize, however, that while these numbers are impressive, we anticipate even greater success in the years ahead.

Ed Willer

Ed Willer
York Properties, Inc.
Raleigh, North Carolina
1992 Treasurer, RELO

1990 NETWORK SALES
in $ Billions

C-21 68   RELO 60   RE/MAX 49   Coldwell Banker 47   Prudential 29   ERA 23

STEP 8: THE MAPS

For the maps in the background, Rice took a rough line drawing of a map of the United States, scanned it, and opened the scan as a template in Illustrator. Then she created a cleaner, more graphic version in Illustrator and saved it as an EPS file. Finally she imported the map into XPress, enlarged it to two-page size, and cropped it to the region she needed for each spread. The maps are printed in a special fifth ink, so they had to be printed as spot colors from XPress. To do so, she simply left Process Separations unchecked when she defined the special color in XPress's Colors dialog box. XPress then produced five plates when Rice separated the file.

STEP 9: THE WAVE PATTERN

Rice created the wave pattern for the water areas of the maps as a patterned fill in FreeHand. She filled a page-size object with FreeHand's predefined zigzag pattern and printed it. Then she enlarged the printout as a stat to 200 percent to widen the space between waves. She scanned the enlarged pattern and printed it at low resolution to maintain the texture. She had the result stripped in mechanically and let the stripper handle any trapping problems.

Comping on Special Paper

You don't have to wait for proofs or for your printed publication from the printer to check out your design ideas, even if they require special paper or ink treatments. You can send more than just laser printer/copier paper through a laser printer. Print on acetate sheets to check ideas on transparent overlays or to prepare overhead transparencies for presentations. Vellum, light card stock, and some colored paper also work.

If you don't have a color printer, you can add spot color to your laser printed copies with special colored foil available from Letraset and other companies. You lay one of the foil sheets over the part of the page you want to appear in color, and use a special heating unit—or an iron—to transfer the color to the toner in that area. With tricks like these, you can mimic press techniques when making comps.

STEP 10: THE COMP

Rice prepared color "reader spread" proofs—two-page spreads arranged as a reader would see them—for color approval. She also printed a black-and-white comp of the entire publication, bound like the printed piece would be. To mimic the translucent vellum sheet that appears between the cover and the first and last pages of the brochure, Rice simply ran a sheet of vellum through the laser printer, printing the text reversed out of a marble-patterned vertical bar, to show what the effect would be.

Seybold San Francisco is an annual seminar and trade show devoted to electronic publishing. San Francisco–based OnLine Design publishes a monthly tabloid newsletter on the same subject. For the Fall 1992 show, the Seybold organization asked OnLine Design to produce a daily newspaper covering (and promoting) events at the show.

"Show dailies," as they're called, are a feature of many trade shows, and they're usually ghastly-looking things, crammed with ads and rewritten press releases. The people at OnLine Design wanted to set a new standard, both by producing a handsome publication and by including useful stories and interviews along with the daily listings of speakers and events. They used the cover of the newspaper to plug the stories inside and induce show attendees to pick up the paper, read it, and maybe even save it. They also varied the color scheme with each day's issue, so harried showgoers would notice that there was a different issue every day.

Seybold San Francisco
Show Daily
Designer: John Sullivan &
Dennis Gallagher/
Visual Strategies
Hardware: Apple
Macintosh IIcx and
IIci, Apple 13-inch
color and Radius full-
page monochrome
monitors, SuperMac
24-bit color card,
Microtek 600ZS scan-
ner, Apple LaserWriter
II, QMS ColorScript
color thermal printer
Software: QuarkXPress
3.1, Adobe Photoshop
2.0.1, Aldus FreeHand
3.0, Fractal Design
Painter 1.2
Fonts: Olive Nord, Gill
Condensed, Industria,
Glypha, Emigré Modula
Serif

STEP 1: SET UP COLOR BARS

The cover of the newspaper relied on a basic grid that
didn't change from issue to issue: the framework of colored bars surrounding the picture of that issue's interview
subject, and some teaser headlines. The bars are XPress
text boxes filled with a colored background. The color of
the bar on the left changed from day to day to call attention to each new issue.

STEP 2: ADD NAMEPLATE

To create the nameplate, the designers duplicated the purple text box without moving it, using XPress's Step and Repeat command with no offsets specified. They entered the words "SHOW DAILY" in white, set in Emigré's Modula Serif font stretched horizontally to 140 percent of normal size. Then they duplicated the box again, this time moving it over and down one pica with the proper settings in the Step and Repeat dialog box. Next, they changed the color of the text to the same mixture as the purple background, with extra black added to create a shadow. Finally they brought the box with the white type to the front.

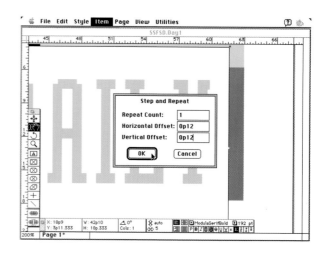

The OnLine Design logo was originally created in FreeHand for use on the monthly tabloid, and saved as an EPS file for import into XPress. To adapt the logo for this application, the words *On Line* were set in Olive Nord and converted to paths. The center of the *O* was removed and replaced by a square, and the letters adjusted for balance and fit. Finally, the word *Design* was added, set in Gill Condensed.

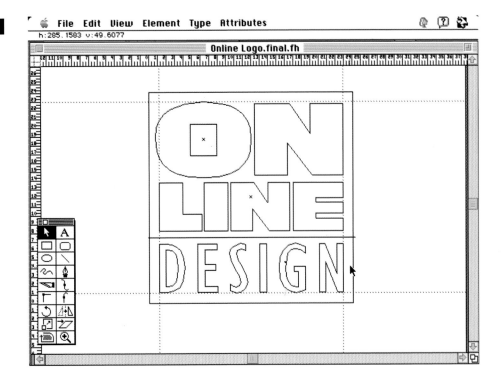

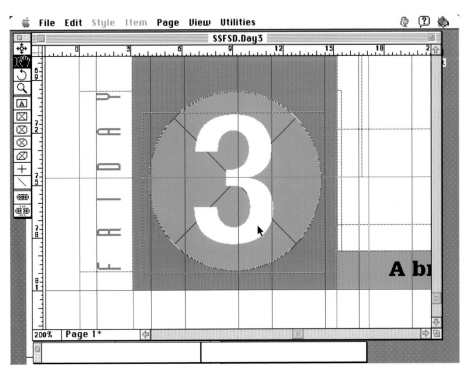

Besides changing the color of the vertical bar, the new issue was also signaled by a bold number in a purple circle. The circle is a picture box in XPress, and the *3* sits in a transparent text box on top of it.

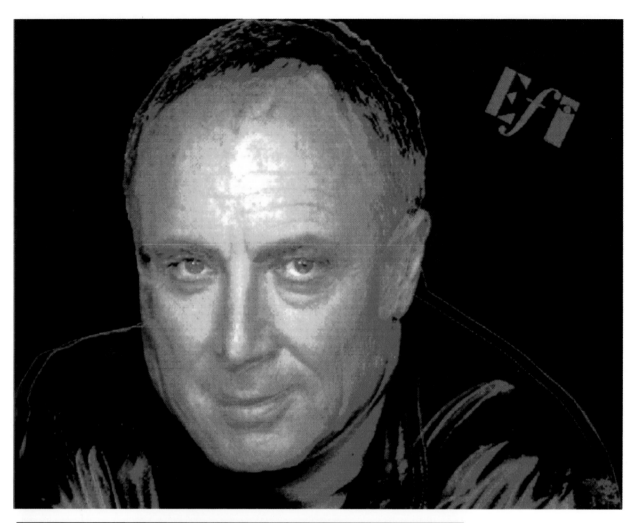

STEP 5: ADD PHOTO

Each issue featured an interview with a notable in the field of electronic publishing, and a prominent cover photo trumpeted the interview. The photo here was scanned by illustrator Diane Fenster as a gray-scale image, then colorized in Photoshop and Painter.

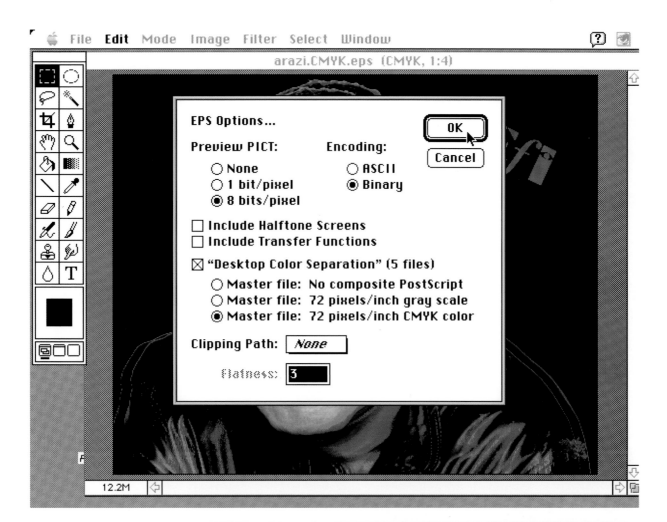

STEP 6: SEPARATE COVER

The colorized photo was saved as an EPS5 file in Photoshop and imported into XPress. The entire cover was then separated with XPress's Print Separations command.

CONFERENCE SESSIONS & SPEAKERS

STEP 7: CREATE INTERIOR HEAD

The page headings throughout the newspaper were created entirely in XPress. The words were typed into a text box, formatted in Glypha, and horizontally scaled to 140 percent. The text box is filled with black and surrounded with a white and black rule using XPress's Frame function; the same feature was used to outline the "Registration Information" box and other such information boxes, with only the weight of the frame changing.

BATTLE OF THE BANDS

◆ ◆ ◆

Creating and Reusing Visuals and a Layout

Commotion 2 is the second in a series of samplers from the Windham Hill Jazz record label. (Visual Strategies also designed the packages for volume one.) The music on the record covers a wide range of styles and moods, so the record company had come up with the name "commotion" to suggest something lively and varied. In their search for an image to communicate the same idea, the designers thought of the old cartoon image of a dog and cat fighting, usually represented as a bunch of shapes swirling in a circle.

The problem arose from the fact that the recording featured several different artists—the designers couldn't rely on a single prominent name to attract shoppers. They had to give emphasis to the names of all the artists to increase the chance that browsers would see a name they liked.

Commotion 2 CD Package
Designer: Dennis Gallagher & John Sullivan/Visual Strategies
Hardware: Apple Macintosh IIcx, Apple 13-inch color and Radius full-page monochrome monitors, SuperMac 24-bit color card, Microtek 600ZS scanner, Apple LaserWriter II, QMS ColorScript color thermal printer
Software: QuarkXPress 3.1, Adobe Photoshop 2.0.1, Aldus FreeHand 3.0, Adobe Illustrator 3.2
Fonts: Berthold City, Adobe OCRB, Zapf Dingbats

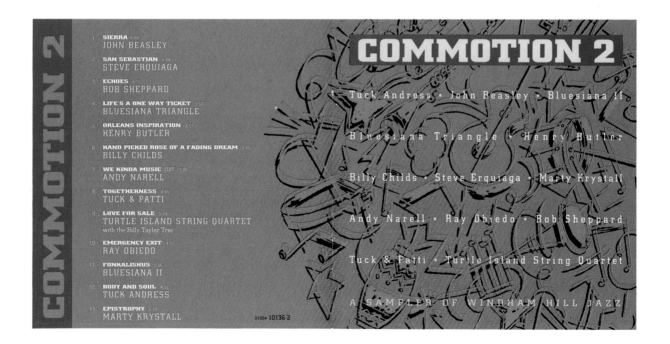

COMMOTION 2 Windham Hill Jazz

0 1934-10136-2 4

COMMOTION 2

Tuck Andress * John Beasley

Bluesiana II * Bluesiana Triangle

Henry Butler * Billy Childs

Steve Erquiaga * Marty Krystall

Andy Narell * Ray Obiedo

Bob Sheppard * Tuck & Patti

Turtle Island String Quartet

A SAMPLER OF WINDHAM HILL JAZZ

Windham Hill Jazz 01934 10136-2

COMMOTION 2 VARIOUS ARTISTS

COMMOTION 2 VARIOUS ARTISTS Windham Hill Jazz 01934 10136-2

STEP 1: CREATE AND SCAN DRAWING

The designers took the dog-and-cat-fight idea and conceived it as a group of musical instruments battling it out. Illustrator Ward Schumaker created an appropriately energetic circular drawing in pen and ink over pencil. The designers scanned the image as line art and brought it into XPress as a TIFF file. But when they placed it on the CD box, the circular shape called attention to the illustration and distracted too much from the artists' names. By enlarging the circle beyond the boundaries of the box, the illustration became a textured background for the names rather than visually competing with them.

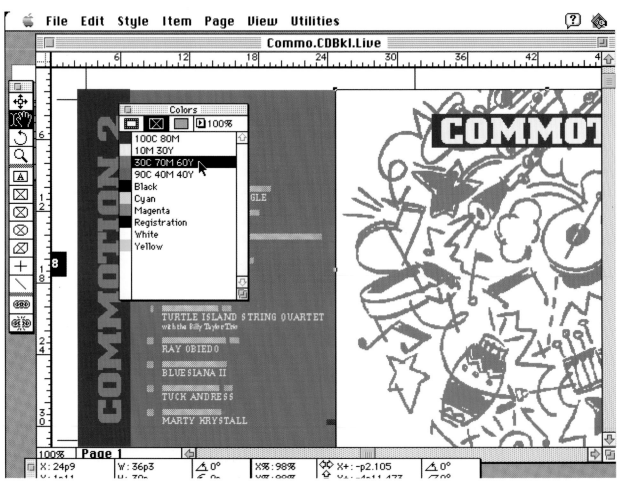

STEP 2: COLOR DRAWING

To create a shadow effect, the designers first filled the background of the graphics box containing the illustration with one CMYK color and used XPress's Colors command to color the drawing with another. Then they duplicated the graphics box in the same place, removed the background color, gave the drawing a new CMYK color, and moved it up and to the right slightly.

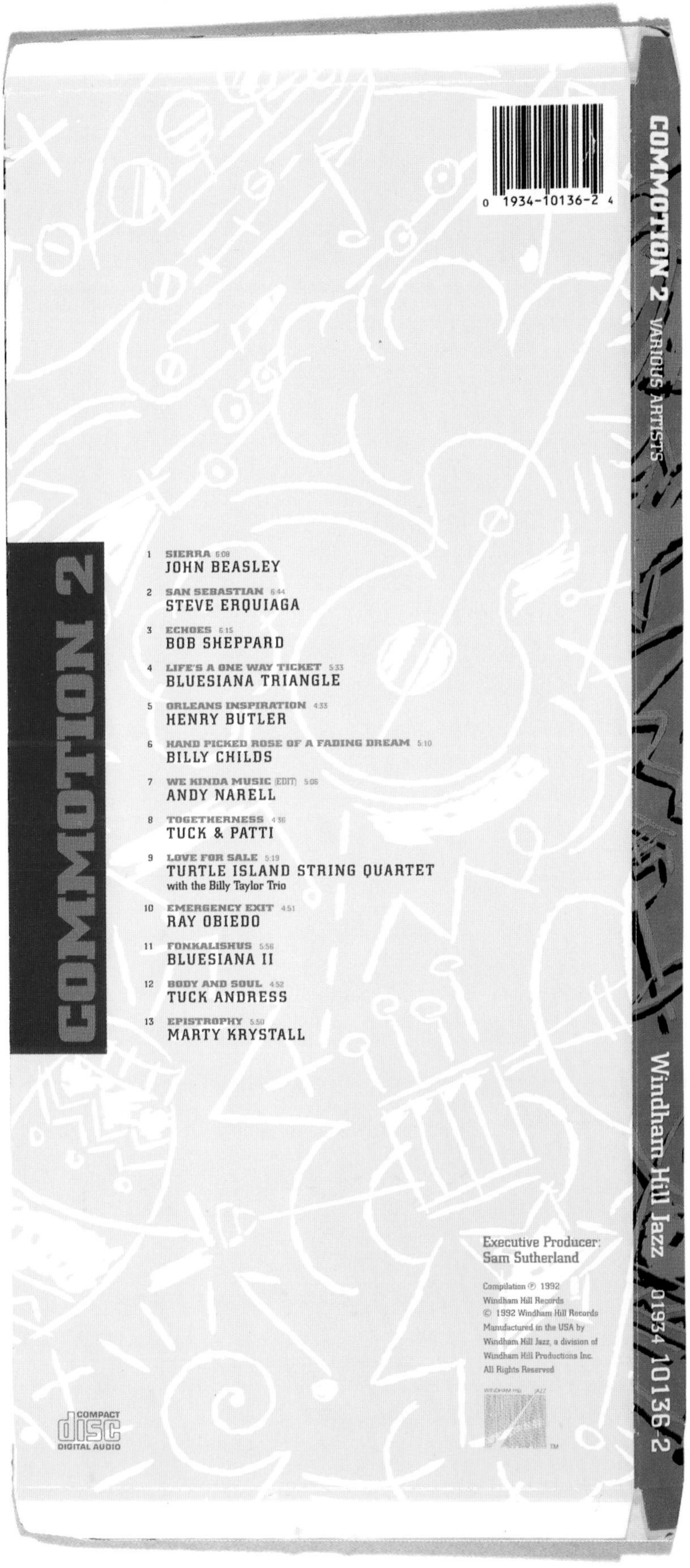
0 1934-10136-2 4
COMMOTION 2 VARIOUS ARTISTS
COMMOTION 2
1 SIERRA 6:09
JOHN BEASLEY
2 SAN SEBASTIAN 6:44
STEVE ERQUIAGA
3 ECHOES 6:15
BOB SHEPPARD
4 LIFE'S A ONE WAY TICKET 5:33
BLUESIANA TRIANGLE
5 ORLEANS INSPIRATION 4:33
HENRY BUTLER
6 HAND PICKED ROSE OF A FADING DREAM 5:10
BILLY CHILDS
7 WE KINDA MUSIC (EDIT) 5:06
ANDY NARELL
8 TOGETHERNESS 4:36
TUCK & PATTI
9 LOVE FOR SALE 5:19
TURTLE ISLAND STRING QUARTET
with the Billy Taylor Trio
10 EMERGENCY EXIT 4:51
RAY OBIEDO
11 FONKALISHUS 5:56
BLUESIANA II
12 BODY AND SOUL 4:52
TUCK ANDRESS
13 EPISTROPHY 5:50
MARTY KRYSTALL
Executive Producer:
Sam Sutherland
Compilation ℗ 1992
Windham Hill Records
© 1992 Windham Hill Records
Manufactured in the USA by
Windham Hill Jazz, a division of
Windham Hill Productions Inc.
All Rights Reserved
COMPACT disc DIGITAL AUDIO
Windham Hill Jazz 01934 10136-2

STEP 3: REDO DRAWING FOR BACK

They wanted to reverse the cover image on the back of the CD box (and on the inside pages of the CD booklet). To create a reversed appearance, the designers simply changed the image color to white and the background to a pale cream—the same color that fills the album name on the front.

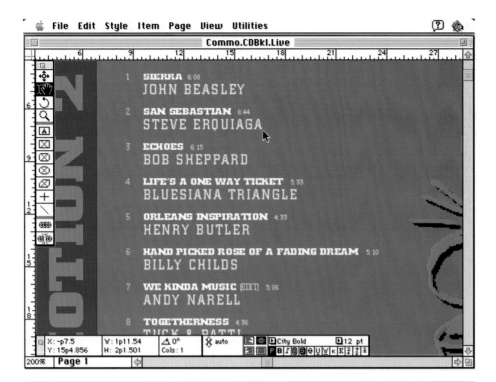

STEP 4: ADD ARTISTS' NAMES

The names of the performers, set in Berthold City, are in a justified text box with no fill, placed over the background illustration. Berthold City's rigid, geometric shapes made a nice contrast to the loose, lively drawing and helped the artists' names stand out from the background. The typeface is also legible at small sizes—its square serifs hold up well— and so proved useful in the CD booklet. The starburst bullets are from Zapf Dingbats, colored the same cream and superscripted by 2 points to move them up from the baseline.

COMMOTION 2

STEP 5: ADD TITLE

For the title, set in a heavier weight of Berthold City, the designers created a text box with a blue background and set the Vertical Alignment to Centered. The type was also centered horizontally and scaled to 130 percent. Last, the word was moved down with the Baseline Shift command until it was visually centered in the box—the mathematical centering obtained with the vertical centering command seldom looks truly centered.

STEP 6: ADD BAR CODES

Visual Strategies placed the bar codes as EPS files. The record company gave them the number and sent them the bar code in EPS format. The numbers, set in Adobe's OCRB font, are part of the EPS file, so Visual Strategies needed to have that font loaded in order for the EPS file to print correctly.

STEP 7: REFORMAT FOR OTHER USES

The CD longbox was the first part of the package designed by Visual Strategies, but it wasn't the only part. They also produced the CD booklet and a cassette insert based on the same design. At the beginning, they considered creating a square image for the CD booklet and just placing it on the longbox and cassette insert. They decided instead to work with some elements that could be rearranged or recropped, rather than just being shrunk, in order to give each part of the package its own identity. They scaled the TIFF files in XPress to enlarge or shrink the background as needed.

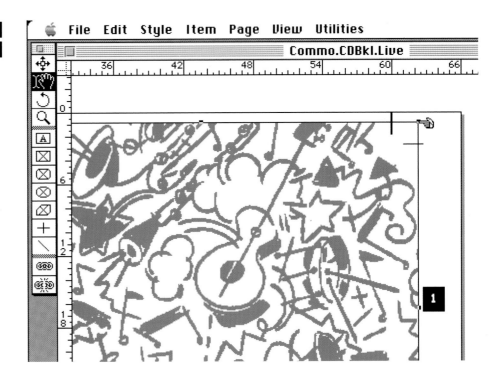

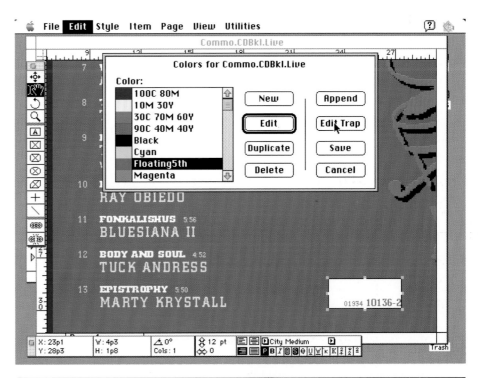

STEP 8: SET UP INTERNATIONAL VERSION

The designers also had to take steps to prepare the package for international distribution. That meant making it easy to remove the label-specific material, the catalog number, and the bar code. In the original U.S. file, those elements are colored white and knock out the background; but for the international market, they were placed on a "floating fifth negative," created by specifying a black spot color. Designers elsewhere could easily suppress the printing of that plate in order to substitute a different catalog number and label name.

ON THE RIGHT TRACK

◆ ◆ ◆

Blending Many Separate Elements Into a Unified Publication

The Bear Treks catalog promotes a collection of tours sponsored by the alumni association of the University of California at Berkeley. The association contracts with several different travel agents to put together the tours; the main design task for the catalog was to bring a lot of disparate elements together into a coherent package.

The design relies on maps to give a quick idea of the content of each tour; photos from previous tours to make the locations seem accessible; and summary boxes to provide the important details. Visual Strategies' biggest challenge was to unify all the different photos so that they complement each other but still give the impression that a variety of experiences are available. The key to solving that problem, and to providing consistency, was a carefully thought-out color scheme, carried through color-coordinated borders, boxes and maps.

Bear Treks Tour Catalog
Designer: John Sullivan &
    Dennis Gallagher/
    Visual Strategies
Hardware: Apple
    Macintosh IIcx, Apple
    13-inch color and
    Radius full-page mono-
    chrome monitors,
    SuperMac 24-bit color
    card, Microtek 600ZS
    scanner, Apple
    LaserWriter II, QMS
    Color Script color ther-
    mal printer
Software: QuarkXPress
    3.1, Adobe Photoshop
    2.0.1, Aldus FreeHand
    3.0, Adobe Illustrator
    3.2
Fonts: Copperplate,
    Helvetica Condensed
    and Compressed, ITC
    Stone Serif

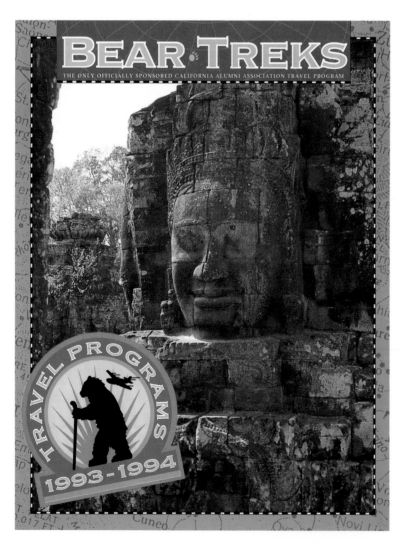

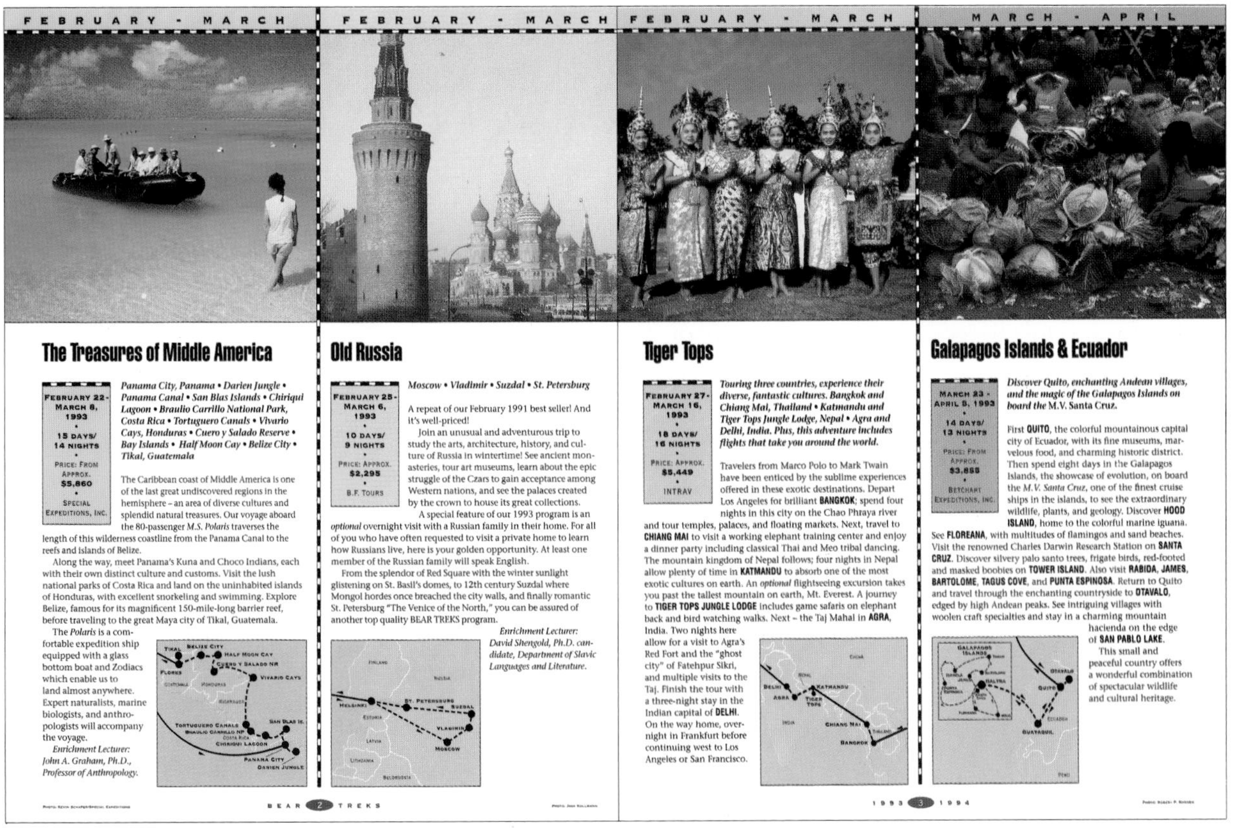

FEBRUARY - MARCH

The Treasures of Middle America

FEBRUARY 22 - MARCH 8, 1993 • 15 DAYS/14 NIGHTS • PRICE: FROM APPROX. $5,860 • SPECIAL EXPEDITIONS, INC.

Panama City, Panama • Darien Jungle • Panama Canal • San Blas Islands • Chiriqui Lagoon • Braulio Carrillo National Park, Costa Rica • Tortuguero Canals • Vivario Cays, Honduras • Cuero y Salado Reserve • Bay Islands • Half Moon Cay • Belize City • Tikal, Guatemala

The Caribbean coast of Middle America is one of the last great undiscovered regions in the hemisphere – an area of diverse cultures and splendid natural treasures. Our voyage aboard the 80-passenger *M.S. Polaris* traverses the length of this wilderness coastline from the Panama Canal to the reefs and islands of Belize.

Along the way, meet Panama's Kuna and Choco Indians, each with their own distinct culture and customs. Visit the lush national parks of Costa Rica and land on the uninhabited islands of Honduras, with excellent snorkeling and swimming. Explore Belize, famous for its magnificent 150-mile-long barrier reef, before traveling to the great Maya city of Tikal, Guatemala.

The *Polaris* is a comfortable expedition ship equipped with a glass bottom boat and Zodiacs which enable us to land almost anywhere. Expert naturalists, marine biologists, and anthropologists will accompany the voyage.

Enrichment Lecturer: John A. Graham, Ph.D., Professor of Anthropology.

FEBRUARY - MARCH

Old Russia

FEBRUARY 25 - MARCH 6, 1993 • 10 DAYS/9 NIGHTS • PRICE: APPROX. $2,295 • B.F. TOURS

Moscow • Vladimir • Suzdal • St. Petersburg

A repeat of our February 1991 best seller! And it's well-priced!

Join an unusual and adventurous trip to study the arts, architecture, history, and culture of Russia in wintertime! See ancient monasteries, tour art museums, learn about the epic struggle of the Czars to gain acceptance among Western nations, and see the palaces created by the crown to house its great collections.

A special feature of our 1993 program is an *optional* overnight visit with a Russian family in their home. For all of you who have often requested to visit a private home to learn how Russians live, here is your golden opportunity. At least one member of the Russian family will speak English.

From the splendor of Red Square with the winter sunlight glistening on St. Basil's domes, to 12th century Suzdal where Mongol hordes once breached the city walls, and finally romantic St. Petersburg "The Venice of the North," you can be assured of another top quality BEAR TREKS program.

Enrichment Lecturer: David Shengold, Ph.D. candidate, Department of Slavic Languages and Literature.

FEBRUARY - MARCH

Tiger Tops

FEBRUARY 27 - MARCH 16, 1993 • 18 DAYS/16 NIGHTS • PRICE: APPROX. $5,449 • INTRAV

Touring three countries, experience their diverse, fantastic cultures. Bangkok and Chiang Mai, Thailand • Katmandu and Tiger Tops Jungle Lodge, Nepal • Agra and Delhi, India. Plus, this adventure includes flights that take you around the world.

Travelers from Marco Polo to Mark Twain have been enticed by the sublime experiences offered in these exotic destinations. Depart Los Angeles for brilliant **BANGKOK**; spend four nights in this city on the Chao Phraya river and tour temples, palaces, and floating markets. Next, travel to **CHIANG MAI** to visit a working elephant training center and enjoy a dinner party including classical Thai and Meo tribal dancing. The mountain kingdom of Nepal follows; four nights in Nepal allow plenty of time in **KATMANDU** to absorb one of the most exotic cultures on earth. An *optional* flightseeing excursion takes you past the tallest mountain on earth, Mt. Everest. A journey to **TIGER TOPS JUNGLE LODGE** includes game safaris on elephant back and bird watching walks. Next – the Taj Mahal in **AGRA**, India. Two nights here allow for a visit to Agra's Red Fort and the "ghost city" of Fatehpur Sikri, and multiple visits to the Taj. Finish the tour with a three-night stay in the Indian capital of **DELHI**. On the way home, overnight in Frankfurt before continuing west to Los Angeles or San Francisco.

MARCH - APRIL

Galapagos Islands & Ecuador

MARCH 23 - APRIL 5, 1993 • 14 DAYS/13 NIGHTS • PRICE: FROM APPROX. $3,855 • BETCHART EXPEDITIONS, INC.

Discover Quito, enchanting Andean villages, and the magic of the Galapagos Islands on board the M.V. Santa Cruz.

First **QUITO**, the colorful mountainous capital city of Ecuador, with its fine museums, marvelous food, and charming historic district. Then spend eight days in the Galapagos Islands, the showcase of evolution, on board the *M.V. Santa Cruz*, one of the finest cruise ships in the islands, to see the extraordinary wildlife, plants, and geology. Discover **HOOD ISLAND**, home to the colorful marine iguana. See **FLOREANA**, with multitudes of flamingos and sand beaches. Visit the renowned Charles Darwin Research Station on **SANTA CRUZ**. Discover silvery palo santo trees, frigate birds, red-footed and masked boobies on **TOWER ISLAND**. Also visit **RABIDA, JAMES, BARTOLOME, TAGUS COVE**, and **PUNTA ESPINOSA**. Return to Quito and travel through the enchanting countryside to **OTAVALO**, edged by high Andean peaks. See intriguing villages with woolen craft specialties and stay in a charming mountain hacienda on the edge of **SAN PABLO LAKE**.

This small and peaceful country offers a wonderful combination of spectacular wildlife and cultural heritage.

BEAR 2 TREKS — 1993 3 1994

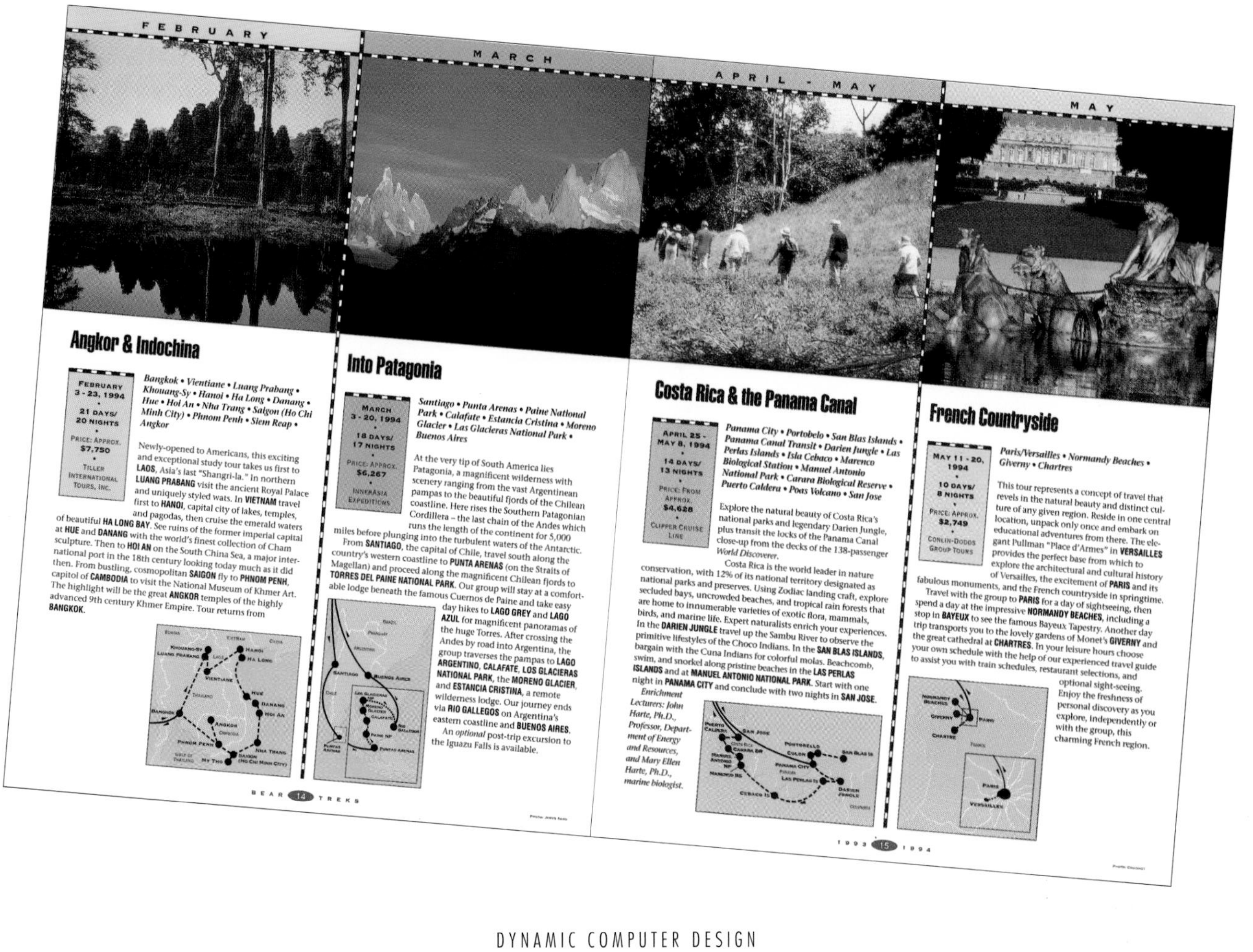

FEBRUARY

Angkor & Indochina

FEBRUARY 3 - 23, 1994 • 21 DAYS/20 NIGHTS • PRICE: APPROX. $7,750 • TILLER INTERNATIONAL TOURS, INC.

Bangkok • Vientiane • Luang Prabang • Khouang-Sy • Hanoi • Ha Long • Danang • Hue • Hoi An • Nha Trang • Saigon (Ho Chi Minh City) • Phnom Penh • Siem Reap • Angkor

Newly-opened to Americans, this exciting and exceptional study tour takes us first to **LAOS**, Asia's last "Shangri-la." In northern **LUANG PRABANG** visit the ancient Royal Palace and uniquely styled wats. In **VIETNAM** travel first to **HANOI**, capital city of lakes, temples, and pagodas, then cruise the emerald waters of beautiful **HA LONG BAY**. See ruins of the former imperial capital at **HUE** and **DANANG** with the world's finest collection of Cham sculpture. Then to **HOI AN** on the South China Sea, a major international port in the 18th century looking today much as it did then. From bustling, cosmopolitan **SAIGON** fly to **PHNOM PENH**, capital of **CAMBODIA** to visit the National Museum of Khmer Art. The highlight will be the great **ANGKOR** temples of the highly advanced 9th century Khmer Empire. Tour returns from **BANGKOK**.

MARCH

Into Patagonia

MARCH 3 - 20, 1994 • 18 DAYS/17 NIGHTS • PRICE: APPROX. $6,267 • INNERASIA EXPEDITIONS

Santiago • Punta Arenas • Paine National Park • Calafate • Estancia Cristina • Moreno Glacier • Las Glacieras National Park • Buenos Aires

At the very tip of South America lies Patagonia, a magnificent wilderness with scenery ranging from the vast Argentinean pampas to the beautiful fjords of the Chilean coastline. Here rises the Southern Patagonian Cordillera – the last chain of the Andes which runs the length of the continent for 5,000 miles before plunging into the turbulent waters of the Antarctic.

From **SANTIAGO**, the capital of Chile, travel south along the country's western coastline to **PUNTA ARENAS** (on the Straits of Magellan) and proceed along the magnificent Chilean fjords to **TORRES DEL PAINE NATIONAL PARK**. Our group will stay at a comfortable lodge beneath the famous Cuernos de Paine and take easy day hikes to **LAGO GREY** and **LAGO AZUL** for magnificent panoramas of the huge Torres. After crossing the Andes by road into Argentina, the group traverses the pampas to **LAGO ARGENTINO, CALAFATE, LOS GLACIERAS NATIONAL PARK**, the **MORENO GLACIER**, and **ESTANCIA CRISTINA**, a remote wilderness lodge. Our journey ends via **RIO GALLEGOS** on Argentina's eastern coastline and **BUENOS AIRES**.

An *optional* post-trip excursion to the Iguazu Falls is available.

APRIL - MAY

Costa Rica & the Panama Canal

APRIL 25 - MAY 8, 1994 • 14 DAYS/13 NIGHTS • PRICE: FROM APPROX. $4,628 • CLIPPER CRUISE LINE

Panama City • Portobelo • San Blas Islands • Panama Canal Transit • Darien Jungle • Las Perlas Islands • Isla Cebaco • Marenco Biological Station • Manuel Antonio National Park • Carara Biological Reserve • Puerto Caldera • Poas Volcano • San Jose

Explore the natural beauty of Costa Rica's national parks and legendary Darien Jungle, plus transit the locks of the Panama Canal close-up from the decks of the 138-passenger *World Discoverer*.

Costa Rica is the world leader in nature conservation, with 12% of its national territory designated as national parks and preserves. Using Zodiac landing craft, explore secluded bays, uncrowded beaches, and tropical rain forests that are home to innumerable varieties of exotic flora, mammals, birds, and marine life. Expert naturalists enrich your experiences. In the **DARIEN JUNGLE** travel up the Sambu River to observe the primitive lifestyles of the Choco Indians. In the **SAN BLAS ISLANDS**, bargain with the Cuna Indians for colorful molas. Beachcomb, swim, and snorkel along pristine beaches in the **LAS PERLAS ISLANDS** and at **MANUEL ANTONIO NATIONAL PARK**. Start with one night in **PANAMA CITY** and conclude with two nights in **SAN JOSE**.

Enrichment Lecturers: John Harte, Ph.D., Professor, Department of Energy and Resources, and Mary Ellen Harte, Ph.D., marine biologist.

MAY

French Countryside

MAY 11 - 20, 1994 • 10 DAYS/8 NIGHTS • PRICE: APPROX. $2,749 • CONLIN-DODDS GROUP TOURS

Paris/Versailles • Normandy Beaches • Giverny • Chartres

This tour represents a concept of travel that revels in the natural beauty and distinct culture of any given region. Reside in one central location, unpack only once and embark on educational adventures from there. The elegant Pullman "Place d'Armes" in **VERSAILLES** provides the perfect base from which to explore the architectural and cultural history of Versailles, the excitement of **PARIS** and its fabulous monuments, and the French countryside in springtime.

Travel with the group to **PARIS** for a day of sightseeing, then spend a day at the impressive **NORMANDY BEACHES**, including a stop in **BAYEUX** to see the famous Bayeux Tapestry. Another day trip transports you to the lovely gardens of Monet's **GIVERNY** and the great cathedral at **CHARTRES**. In your leisure hours choose your own schedule with the help of our experienced travel guide to assist you with train schedules, restaurant selections, and optional sight-seeing.

Enjoy the freshness of personal discovery as you explore, independently or with the group, this charming French region.

BEAR 14 TREKS — 1993 15 1994

DYNAMIC COMPUTER DESIGN

107

STEP 1: DETERMINE PALETTE OF COLORS

The first thing Visual Strategies did was determine the palette of colors for the tinted boxes and bars on the pages. The designers made color pencil sketches, then matched the colors as closely as possible with CMYK percentages from a color reference book. They used XPress's Colors command to make a palette of the colors under consideration; then they created a grid of text boxes, filled each one with a different color from the palette, and labeled them. They separated the page and made a composite proof, then selected the final colors from it and deleted the unwanted colors from XPress's color palette.

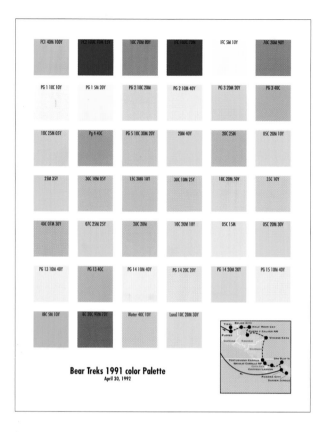

Bear Treks 1991 color Palette
April 30, 1992

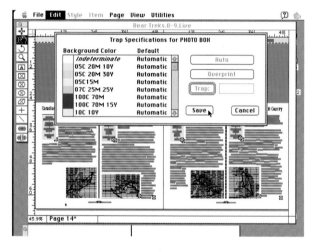

STEP 2: MAKE ROOM FOR PHOTOS

The photos, in transparency form, were scanned on a Hell drum scanner and separated to the final size. At the same time, the designers made low-resolution gray-scale scans of the transparencies on their flatbed scanner—with a transparency attachment—and used them for positioning and cropping. The gray-scale images were eventually replaced with black windows and the Hell separations stripped in traditionally.

The designers created windows for the photos by setting up a fifth color as a spot color so it would separate as a fifth negative. That way they could trap the window to the other colors on the page with XPress's automatic trapping function. Also, if the window had been created on the black plate, as is usually the case, it would butt up against the black segments of the dashed "railroad" rules, creating further stripping problems.

STEP 3: SCAN MAPS

The designers turned to a standard atlas for the maps, photocopying them at roughly the same size. Then they traced the necessary details by hand, onto tracing paper, and scanned the results.

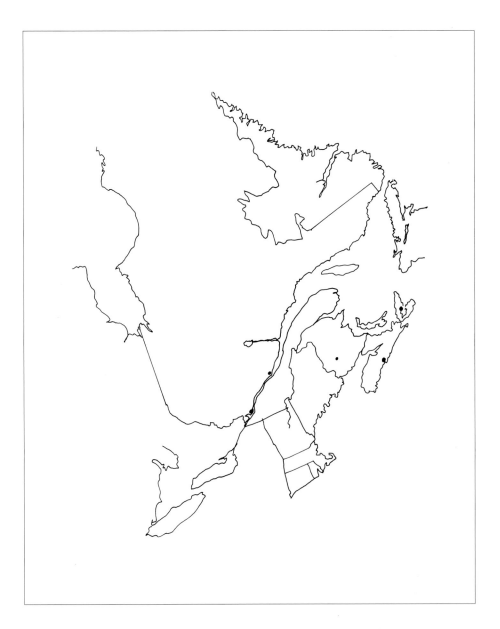

STEP 4: DRAW MAPS

The designers loaded the scanned tracings into Illustrator and drew over them to create the final simplified line-art maps. To match the colors they had selected, they recreated color definitions from the XPress palettes to tint the maps in Illustrator, added the route markings, and saved the results as EPS files for import into XPress.

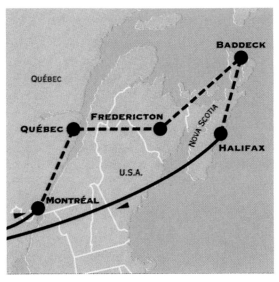

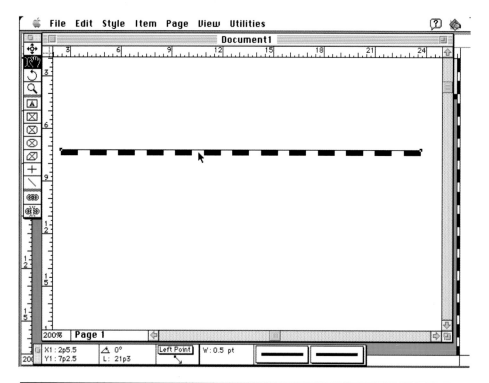

STEP 5: CREATE DOTTED LINES

The "railroad line," used as a graphic divider and border throughout the catalog, was created entirely in XPress. The designers first drew a dashed line 4 points wide. Then they duplicated that line twice, changed the width of each duplicate to .5 points, and turned them into solid lines. Next, they moved one thin line up 2 points and the other down 2 points to close off the edges of the dashed line. Finally, they grouped the three lines so they could duplicate, angle and place them as needed.

STEP 6: CREATE NAMEPLATE

The "Bear Treks" nameplate was created in FreeHand out of Copperplate type, using the Inline type effect to fill the letters with gold and outline them in white. The longitude/latitude lines behind the words are also part of the FreeHand file. The logo was exported as an EPS file and placed into XPress, with a transparent text box placed over it to hold the "Only Officially Sponsored" subhead.

The "luggage sticker" emblem was also created in FreeHand, by placing Copperplate text, with the same colors as the nameplate, on a path around a drawing. It was imported into XPress and rotated there.

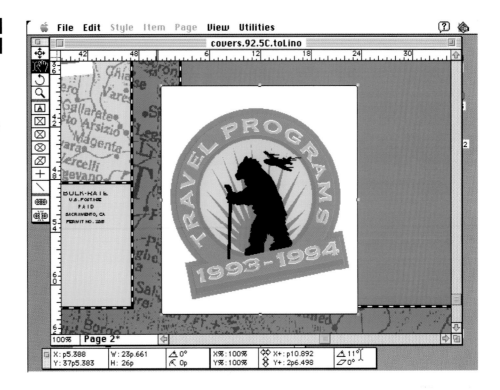

STEP 8: PLACE MAP BORDER

The map borders and background were scanned from one of the map photocopies and brought into XPress as a TIFF file. The colors were added in XPress.

HIGH-TECH SOPHISTICATION

◆ ◆ ◆

Scanning for Art and Electronic Typesetting

The people at Digital Video Applications Corporation knew they had a nifty product, and they wanted the rest of the world to know it too. Their Video-Shop was going to be one of the first programs to work with Apple Computer's new QuickTime video data format. They came to Michael Sullivan's design firm, Imprimatur, because of his expertise in helping to roll out new software.

DiVA already had some promotional material from their Japanese distributor, but it had a glossy, technological look. Sullivan felt strongly that they had to give VideoShop a more artsy, elegant image, because the intended market was art directors and other creative types. Those people don't want more technology; they want creative tools.

DiVA needed a package design—even though the software was still in development—so the ad campaign could start. After presenting several different concepts, Sullivan finally persuaded the company to agree to an "album cover" approach, based on an allegorical image and visionary feel.

DiVA VideoShop Package
Designer: Michael
    Sullivan/Imprimatur
    Design
Hardware: Apple
    Macintosh IIci's (sev-
    eral), 19-inch monitors
    (different manufactur-
    ers), 24-bit graphics
    boards (different man-
    ufacturers), Varityper
    VT600W 600-dpi laser
    printer, Apple
    LaserWriter IINTX,
    Mitsubishi 650 color
    printer
Software: Atex
    Renaissance, Aldus
    FreeHand, Adobe
    Photoshop, Custom
    Applications, Inc.'s
    Freedom of Press
Fonts: Avenir Book and
    Bold, Odeon
    Condensed, Kunstler
    Script, Helvetica
    Condensed, Linotype
    Linoscript

Part I: The Logo

STEP 1: DEVELOP THE CONCEPT

DiVA already had chosen a typeface for the company logo and wanted Sullivan to use the same face for the text on the package. Sullivan, though, wanted to separate the company identity from the product identity to keep the focus on the audience's artistic bent. He also wanted a complete logo for the product, not just a type treatment of its name, to reinforce its appeal as an artistic tool. He decided to split apart the three words of the product name—"DiVA," "Video" and "Shop"—and highlight the one that really cut to the nature of the product, "Video."

STEP 2: DRAW FILM ICON

Videotape doesn't have sprocket holes, of course, but a piece of film was still the obvious choice to quickly get across what VideoShop does. (Apple chose a similar icon to represent a QuickTime movie.) The icon was created in Aldus FreeHand by drawing a black-filled rectangle for the film and several squares with no line or fill for the holes inside it. After using the Ungroup command on the rectangle and holes, Sullivan selected them all and chose the Join Elements command. That turned the squares into true holes in the black rectangle—rather than transparent boxes lying on it—that any background would show through.

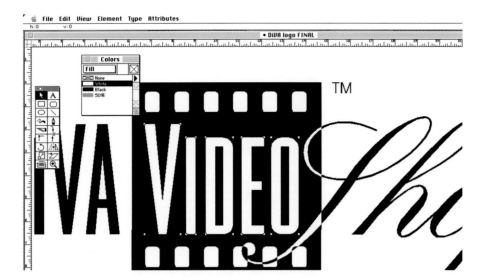

STEP 3: FORMAT "VIDEO"

The word "Video" is simply colored white and placed over the black rectangle. The type-face for "Video" (and "DiVA") is Odeon Condensed: Sullivan wanted something that would appeal to those art directors, and Odeon Condensed is trendy these days. The typeface also has no lowercase letters, making it a good match for the caps/small caps treatment the company uses for its trademark.

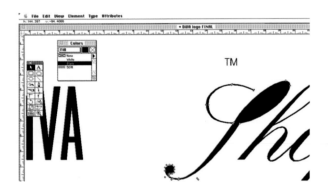

STEP 4: FORMAT "SHOP"

Sullivan decided to balance the trendy parts of the logo with a more traditionally artistic treatment of the word "Shop." He set it in Kunstler Script, extending the bottom of the *S* to intersect the film icon. To do this, he used the Convert to Paths command with the type selected and edited the outline just like any other FreeHand graphic element.

STEP 5: ADD "SHOP" TO LOGO

Where the *S* crosses into the film icon, it changes color—it's actually white, not a hole in the black like the sprocket holes. Sullivan achieved the effect using FreeHand's Paste Inside feature, which lets one object act as a "cookie cut-ter" so another object can show through. Sullivan selected the *S* and cloned it, creating a duplicate on top of the original *S*. Then he filled the duplicate with white and, without moving it, cut it to the Clipboard. He selected the black rectangle and chose Paste Inside. The part of the white let-ter that overlapped the rectangle became in essence, part of the rectangle's fill.

Part II: The Photo

For the cover photo, Sullivan wanted to get away from high-tech graphics by using a more painterly image that would have a soft quality often missing from digital images. The name *diva* suggested a picture of a woman, but instead of the typical, exploitative "beautiful girl" shot, he wanted one of a woman with a combination of strength and sensuality.

The image was created with two shots. First the model was photographed in black and white, standing on a stepladder with her head back and the camera at an angle to suggest flight. Next, the photographer made a 16 x 20-inch print of the photo, put a slit in it, and fed a strip of film through the slit. Then he photographed that assembly to get the final image. The color was added through creative darkroom techniques.

STEP 2: ADD NOTES

Sullivan added the musical notes in Photoshop. He had the photo scanned on a Scitex system and saved in Scitex CT format, which Photoshop can open. In Photoshop, he used the text tool to type characters from Carta, a font of musical and other symbols, into a separate channel. Then he loaded the note outlines as selections and copied and moved the selected area of the photo, so the color of each note would be a color from somewhere else in the image.

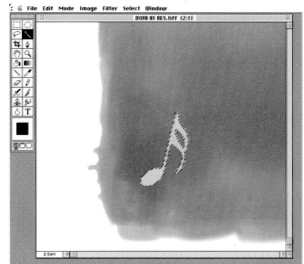

Working With a Scitex System

The term "Scitex system" loosely refers to a combination of a high-end drum scanner, a computer console the size of a large drafting table, proprietary image-editing software, and a high-resolution film recorder. (Similar systems are made by Linotype-Hell and DuPont-Crosfield.) Such systems represent the state of the art for photo enhancement, special effects and color separation. Like imagesetters, they're expensive pieces of equipment (costing hundreds of thousands of dollars) that require trained operators, and most publishers who want to use the Scitex system contract their color work to a color separation house, paying for the service by the hour.

There are ways you can take advantage of Scitex's capabilities while doing the work yourself, though, which lets you experiment without paying for someone else's time. For example, drum scanners capture color and contrast much better than desktop scanners, so if you want to work on an image yourself but want the best scan possible, have one made at a Scitex bureau.

Some software, Adobe Photoshop, for instance, can open a Scitex CT scan file on the Macintosh. Even if the color doesn't look perfect on your monitor, you can be confident that it's correct in the file. If you change the color, you lose that confidence, of course. But if you're using the scan for effects like the musical notes on the VideoShop package, you don't have to worry about the output quality—just save the revised image as a Scitex CT file again for output on a Scitex film recorder.

The main drawback to this approach is the huge size of the file you have to work with—the VideoShop package image was a 30MB file after scanning. That means you need a lot of storage capacity (Sullivan's firm uses a 1-gigabyte—that's 1,000 megabytes—image file server) and fast machines to handle the file.

You can also get a low-res version of the Scitex scan to use as an FPO image in your layout if you're not planning to do any modification of the image yourself. The Scitex operator will then replace your FPO with the high-res original scan during output. This is the concept behind various Mac-to-Scitex links such as Aldus's Open Prepress Interface (OPI)—a standard other programs take advantage of—and QuarkXPress's Visionary link. With this method you don't have to deal with the huge file yourself. If you scale or rotate the photo, though, you'll have to pay for a new scan or for the time required for the Scitex operator to duplicate your changes.

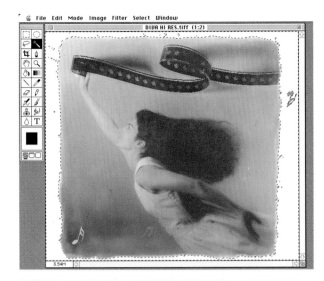

STEP 3: MASK EDGE

On the final print of the photo, the image itself had a jagged edge (from the darkroom techniques used), within the white of the photographic paper. The scanning operation added unwanted dots and pixels in the white border. To clean those up, Sullivan outlined the image with Photoshop's selection tools to mask it, and then erased everything outside the mask.

Part III: The Sell Sheet

STEP 1: DEVELOP THE CONCEPT:
JUST THE HIGH POINTS

The "sell sheet" is a separate piece of paper placed on the back of the box when it's wrapped to explain what the program does. (It's not actually printed on the box because the rest of the box was designed before the program was finished.) The sheet also serves as a promotional flyer.

DiVA wanted to take the feature-list approach, but Sullivan convinced them that their market would respond better to an explanation of benefits. On the left, the main column of copy—written by DiVA but embellished by Sullivan—describes what the program can do; on the right, four screen shots outline specific features.

*I*n today's competitive environment, the message that stands out is the one that counts. Video – no other medium allows you to communicate so much, so compellingly, so distinctively. And no other software allows you to work with video as quickly, easily, or intuitively as DiVA VideoShop.

VideoShop marries powerful digital video technology with a friendly Macintosh interface to produce the complete software solution for creating, editing, and presenting QuickTime movies. Best of all, you don't have to be a video editor to use VideoShop. If you know how to use a Macintosh – how to select, cut, paste, drag, and drop – you have all the skills you need to become an expert QuickTime movie maker.

LET YOUR IMAGINATION RUN WILD

VideoShop lets you quickly visualize, refine, and realize creative concepts. Brainstorming becomes easy with VideoShop's powerful built-in recording and storyboarding capabilities.

EXPRESS YOURSELF

VideoShop's multi-track functionality allows you to lay out multiple media elements on the screen to create exciting multimedia business presentations. Your graphs, slides, and charts will take on a new meaning when enhanced with video, animation, and audio to create compelling messages that can be output to videotape, or played back on the computer.

EFFORTLESSLY

VideoShop's seamless integration with HyperCard® makes incorporating video into your educational and training stacks effortless. Drag and drop a movie icon from a visual folder onto a card. Click on the micon, and the associated movie is played back. There's no scripting involved!

Regardless of the application, Video-Shop will forever enhance the way you communicate.

System Requirements (minimum)
Macintosh LC, Si, Macintosh II, or Quadra family; 4 MB RAM (8 MB recommended); 40 MB hard disc. System 7.0 or later (functionality limited under system 6.0.7); 32-bit QuickDraw; QuickTime; Claris HyperCard 2.1 (included in box). Adobe® Photoshop® plug-in filters supported. QuickTime-compatible video board for live video capture; no special hardware required for playback.

THE QUICKTIME® MOVIE CREATION, EDITING & PRESENTATION TOOL FOR THE MACINTOSH™

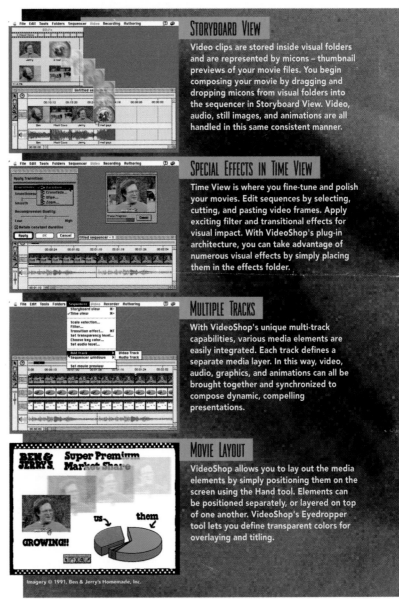

Imagery © 1991, Ben & Jerry's Homemade, Inc.

STORYBOARD VIEW

Video clips are stored inside visual folders and are represented by micons – thumbnail previews of your movie files. You begin composing your movie by dragging and dropping micons from visual folders into the sequencer in Storyboard View. Video, audio, still images, and animations are all handled in this same consistent manner.

SPECIAL EFFECTS IN TIME VIEW

Time View is where you fine-tune and polish your movies. Edit sequences by selecting, cutting, and pasting video frames. Apply exciting filter and transitional effects for visual impact. With VideoShop's plug-in architecture, you can take advantage of numerous visual effects by simply placing them in the effects folder.

MULTIPLE TRACKS

With VideoShop's unique multi-track capabilities, various media elements are easily integrated. Each track defines a separate media layer. In this way, video, audio, graphics, and animations can all be brought together and synchronized to compose dynamic, compelling presentations.

MOVIE LAYOUT

VideoShop allows you to lay out the media elements by simply positioning them on the screen using the Hand tool. Elements can be positioned separately, or layered on top of one another. VideoShop's Eyedropper tool lets you define transparent colors for overlaying and titling.

DiVA Corporation

222 Third Street
Cambridge, Massachusetts 02142
(617) 491-4147

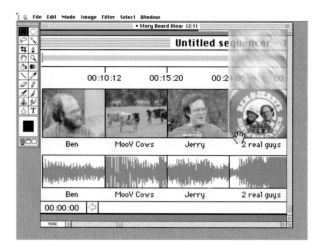

STEP 2: ACQUIRE SCREEN SHOTS

The screen shots come from a multimedia sequence developed by the Ben & Jerry's ice cream company for in-store display. Sullivan brought them as PICT files into Photoshop. By copying and pasting parts of the image and then applying a Motion Blur to the copies, he was able to suggest motion and action.

STEP 3: ADD BACKGROUND

The background for the screen shots is a detail of the model's hand from the front photo, blown up in Photoshop many times until the pixels are visible. Atex Renaissance lets you paste an image into any object on the screen; Sullivan also dropped part of the photo into the circle behind the drop cap.

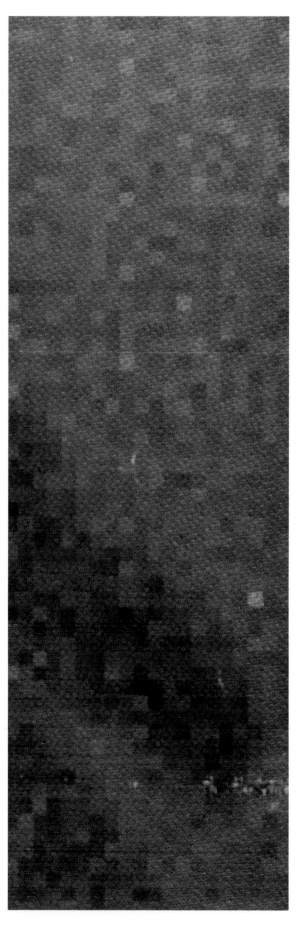

*I*n today'... ment, th... out is th... Video – r... you to com... compellingly, so c... other software all... video as quickly, e... DiVA VideoShop.

STEP 4: FORMAT COPY

All the text is formatted with Renaissance style sheets. Sullivan wanted a simple, clean typeface that would work with the Odeon heads without calling attention to itself. He felt a sans serif face would be best and chose Avenir (regular and bold), a nice compromise between the personality of Futura and the plainness of Helvetica and Univers.

For the drop cap, Sullivan wanted a script face to pick up on the Kunstler Script used for the word "Shop." The Kunstler *I* is so slanted, though, that it would have been unrecognizable standing alone, so Sullivan chose Linoscript instead, a more vertical, formal script face.

STEP 5: ASSEMBLE AND PRINT

Sullivan also used Renaissance to assemble the elements for the rest of the package—the logo, cover image and text. On the sides of the box, he chose the simple, direct Helvetica Condensed for the type.

The early version of Renaissance that Sullivan had couldn't make four-color separations of the screen shots, so he had to find a workaround. (Later versions accept Desktop Color Separation [DCS] files, which means they can print separations using preseparated TIFF files from programs like Photoshop.) First he printed the Renaissance page to disk as a PostScript file. He then processed that file with Adobe Separator (the separation utility for Adobe Illustrator), which created a PostScript file with the separation information encoded in it. He sent the separated file to the Scitex system, whose operator turned the whole sheet into a huge, high-resolution bitmap held in the Scitex computer's memory. The Scitex operator was able to cut out the part of the bitmap where the screen shots were and replace them with Scitex CT versions of the screen—just as you would cut and paste in MacPaint—for final output on the Scitex Dolev film recorder.

WELL-SET TABLES

❖ ❖ ❖

Typesetting Tables and Other Production Chores Made Easy

Aeroflot: *An Airline and its Aircraft* is the fourth in a series of airline histories written by R.E.G. Davies and published by Paladwr Press. Brian Day and Kimberly Fisher had worked on the previous volume, about Delta Airlines, and were tapped to produce the Aeroflot volume as well.

The books' design formats were pretty well set—they're designed by the author, who's based at the Smithsonian's Air and Space Museum—so Fisher & Day's job was mainly one of typesetting and production. The maps were created by Davies and the aircraft illustrations hand-drawn by Mike Machat; both were separated and stripped in traditionally. The photographs were also handled by traditional means. But the airline book presented several interesting challenges, mostly in typesetting the large number of tables it contains.

Aeroflot: An Airline and
    Its Aircraft
Designer: Kimberly Fisher
    and Pat Woodward/
    Fisher & Day
Hardware: Apple
    Macintosh II, Abaton
    Scan 300/GS gray-scale
    scanner, Apple
    LaserWriter Plus
Software: QuarkXPress
Fonts: Clearface Gothic,
    ITC, Stone Serif,
    Univers 47 Condensed,
    Zapf Dingbats

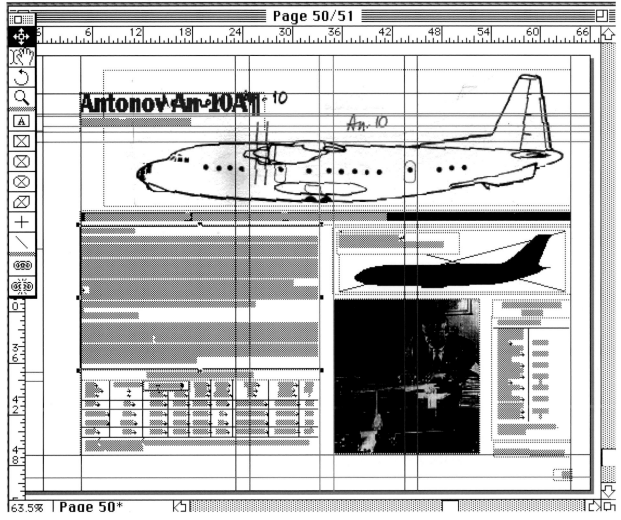

63.5% | Page 50*

STEP 1: CREATE MASTER PAGE

The first step in formatting the book was to set up a basic layout for both left- and right-hand pages. Fisher and Woodward set up master pages in XPress with a three-column grid, defined with the Master Guides command (the blue vertical guidelines in the figure). Then they manually added an extra set of ruler guides to divide the right-hand page into two equal columns. The master pages also contain most of the horizontal guidelines (the green lines) that determine the placement of the headlines and the large airplane picture.

With the guidelines established, the designers simply drew the required number of text and graphics boxes to fit. The author sent the text on disk to the managing editor in rural California, who in turn sent it to Fisher and Day in San Francisco. They flowed text into XPress and formatted it, often requesting the editor to edit the text to fit.

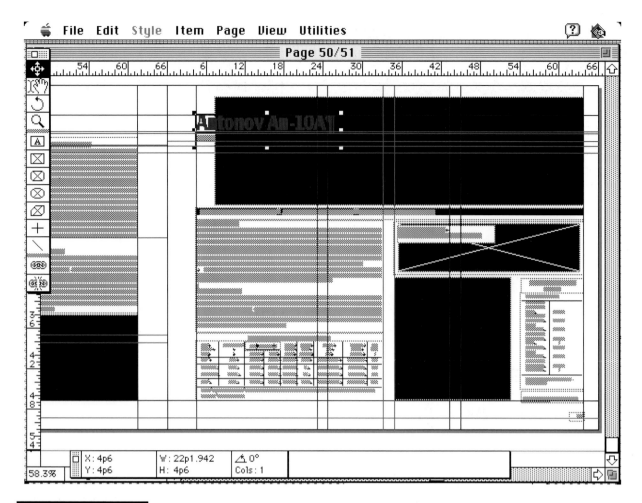

STEP 2: ADD PICTURES

The designers worked with photocopies and faxes of the artwork and photos, scanning them for the layout. They ultimately replaced the scans with black windows before going to film and had the printer strip in traditional halftones and separations.

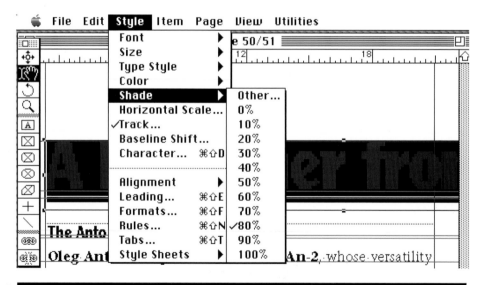

STEP 3: COLOR HEADLINE

The two headlines are printed in a dark gray, created by leaving them in the default black color but choosing 80 percent from the Shade menu.

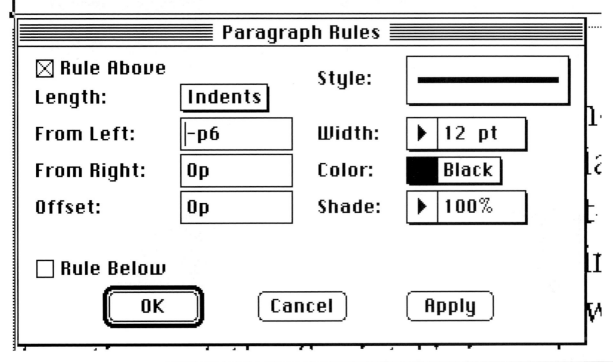

Ivchenko AI-20K (4 x 4,00

Paragraph Rules

☒ **Rule Above**

Length: [Indents]

From Left: [-p6]

From Right: [0p]

Offset: [0p]

Style: [———]

Width: ▶ [12 pt]

Color: ■ [Black]

Shade: ▶ [100%]

☐ **Rule Below**

[OK] [Cancel] [Apply]

STEP 4: FORMAT INFO BAR

The designers used XPress's Rules command to create the reversed-out text for the air-craft information bar. First they defined a Rule Above that was thicker than the height of the type (a 12-point rule over 10-point text), and then they used the Baseline Shift command to move the text up over the bar. Finally they colored the text white. That way, a reversed-type effect became part of the paragraph format, so the designers could save it in the style sheet and easily repeat the effect elsewhere.

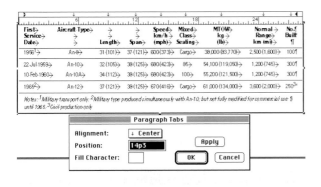

STEP 5: SET UP TABS

The first step in creating the table of aircraft features was to set the tabs that define the columns. With the exception of the leftmost column, the designers decided to center all the table entries.

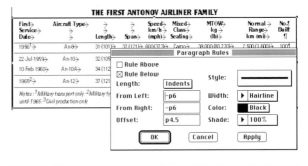

STEP 6: ADD RULES

For the horizontal lines in the table, the designers were able to use XPress's Rules feature again to define thin rules below certain lines of text. The whole table is one big text box, so they were able to use the Frame command to put a rule around it.

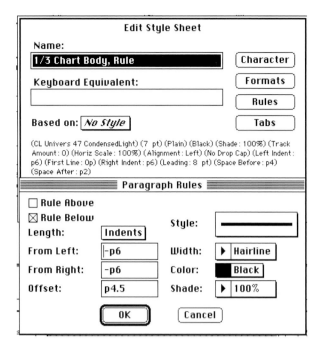

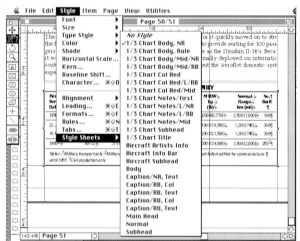

STEP 7: SAVE STYLES

By creating as many rules as possible with paragraph formatting commands, the designers could save the settings as paragraph styles and quickly use them in all the other tables in the book. There's basically a table or two on every spread, so that saved a lot of formatting time.

Working With Tabular Material

In the words of Kimberly Fisher, "Tabular material is not much fun to work with." Some programs, such as Ventura Publisher and FrameMaker (and even later versions of Microsoft Word and Word for Windows), have built-in table-making functions, which can simplify the process enormously. Aldus PageMaker comes with a separate Table Editor program for setting up tables that can be imported into PageMaker. And for QuarkXPress, you can get an XTension for making tables.

Even with these programs, however, you will likely make some tables the old-fashioned way, by arranging columns with tab settings. Here are a few tips to make the process easier:

◆ Always set up exactly the tab stops you need, rather than relying on the default ruler settings, which in most programs set a tab stop every half inch. The basic principle is: Use as few tabs as possible. With custom tabs, you only have to tab once to get to the place you want; but if you leave the default tabs, you may end up tabbing several times to get there. Each tab then becomes a separate character in the middle of your text. All those extra tabs can cause problems if you try to reformat the table later.

◆ Programs generally let you choose from four types of tabs: left, right, center and decimal. Use right-aligned tab stops for columns of numbers with no decimals; use the decimal tabs, which line up entries according to periods, for columns of numbers with decimals. XPress also offers comma tabs, which line up entries according to commas, and an Align On feature, which lets you use any character to line up your entries.

◆ Adding false decimal points or dummy characters and coloring them white can help line up numbers. For instance, in a financial table that contains some unadorned numbers and others in parentheses to represent losses, you want to line up all the figures. While XPress knows to "hang" the parentheses, many programs don't. You can add parentheses to numbers that don't have them and color them white; the numbers will then line up correctly. This trick also works for aligning columns in programs that don't have tabs, such as most drawing programs.

Aircraft Type	Dimensions m(ft)		Speed km/h (mph)
	Length	Span	
An-8	31 (101)	37 (121)	600 (373)
An-10	32 (105)	38 (125)	680 (423)
An-10A	34 (112)	38 (125)	680 (423)
An-12	37 (121)	38 (125)	670 (416)

STEP 8: ADD EXTRA TEXT BOXES

Some parts of the tables didn't lend themselves to such neat tricks, however. The "Dimensions" box, for instance, straddles two tabular columns. To run it in with the other text would have required setting up an extra tab stop—or moving an existing tab stop—for that one line. It was easier to create a separate text box and position it by eye.

Fisher and Woodward added the vertical rules in the tables individually, with XPress's line tool. XPress lacks a true table function and so has no concept of a "cell" that can be framed; and while it offers rules above and below a paragraph, it doesn't have any provision for rules beside or around it.

PHOTOGRAPHIC DEVELOPER

◆ ◆ ◆

Electronic Ad Illustration and Production

The newspaper ad for the new Legend Hills residential development was one of a series of promotions Zender + Associates had done for Zaring Homes, Inc., a home-building company. The association between the two firms goes back a long time, and the ad relied on a well-established design system they had worked out over the years, including the two rectangular bars and the photos in the background.

Legend Hills was a neighborhood without houses when the ad was created. Zaring was developing the properties (aimed at fairly upscale second- or third-time home buyers), and buyers could choose the kind of house that would be built on their lot. Designer Priscilla Fisher played off that "Your House Here" idea and came up with the notion of placing one of Zaring's houses into the Legend Hills landscape. She based the ad on two photos taken by Zender's staff photographer, one of a house from another of Zaring's developments, and the other of a Legend Hills landscape.

Clermont County

The block is in.
Be the first one on it.

Visit today for best selection and pricing.

Legend Hills

$209,000 - $279,000

A Master Edition Neighborhood

Special Early Bird pricing is available

Wooded home sites

Only 20 minutes from downtown and airport

Kay Weyrick
7 3 6 . 7 5 9 0

East on Beechmont Avenue, **R** on Nine Mile Road, **L** on Legend Hills

Information Center open 1 - 5:30 except Fridays, and by appointment anytime

the quality builder®
ZARING

Zaring Newspaper Ad
Designer: Priscilla Fisher/
   Zender + Associates,
   Inc.
Hardware: Apple
   Macintosh Quadra 700,
   E-Machines 20-inch
   color monitor, Howtek
   ScanMaster color scan-
   ner with transparency
   scanner, Apple
   LaserWriter II,
   Linotype Linotronic
   300
Software: Aldus FreeHand
   3.1, Adobe Photoshop
   2.0
Fonts: Stempel Garamond,
   Univers family

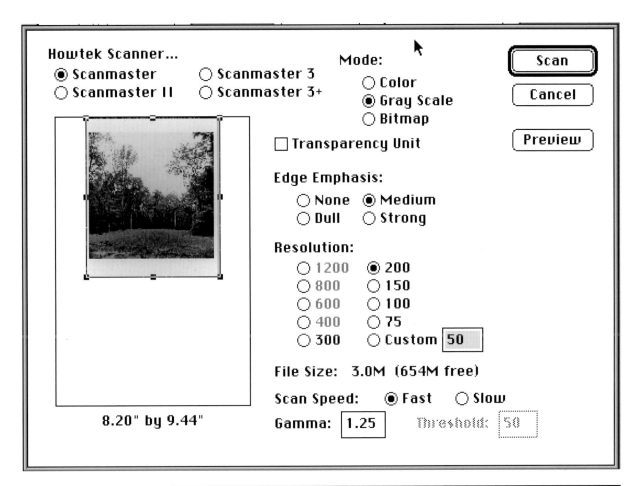

Fisher started by scanning in the two photos using Howtek's plug-in scanning module for Photoshop. The landscape photo was an 8x10 black-and-white print, and the house was a 4x5 color transparency, for which she used the scanner's transparency attachment. She scanned both images at 200 dpi, which gave her more than enough data to get a good halftone at newspaper resolution. She converted the scan of the house to gray-scale in Photoshop and saved both images as TIFF files so she could bring them into FreeHand later.

After scanning the photos, Fisher turned to Photoshop's Levels command to increase the contrast. Based on experience, she knew that higher contrast photos work better for the relatively low-quality reproduction in newspapers. She prefers to work with the Levels rather than the Brightness/Contrast command because it allows for more flexibility in adjusting the tone to the desired result.

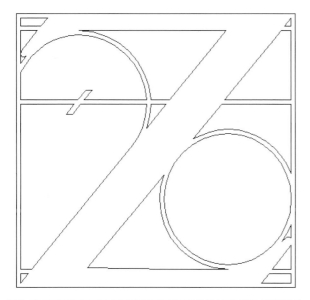

The Zaring logo had been originally drawn in the early '80s, well before the age of electronic design, and subsequently digitized by being scanned and traced in FreeHand. Zender's designers carefully traced all the closed shapes—the Z, the large square, the circles, and so on—with FreeHand's various line drawing tools and then joined them to turn them into closed paths. This enabled the designers to scale the image while accurately preserving its line-weight relationships; they could also create trapping, if needed, by duplicating the objects and changing the stroke weight of the duplicates. They keep the logo as a FreeHand file, copying and pasting it into new documents as needed.

Next, Fisher began to build the layout in FreeHand. She placed the bars and type over a gray rectangle that stood in for the photo to make the work go faster (photos can take a long time to redraw on screen). The black bar and white bar are simply rectangles drawn in FreeHand, with the appropriate fills.

Since there wasn't a lot of copy, she typed it all directly into FreeHand. The large type, set in Stempel Garamond, is all one text block, with the uppermost headline colored white (reversed out of the black bar) and the lower part black. On the other hand, the column of details—set in various members of the Univers family—actually consists of five separate text blocks. Each block contains a separate kind of information. This allowed Fisher to keep similar information together while moving the text boxes around if necessary.

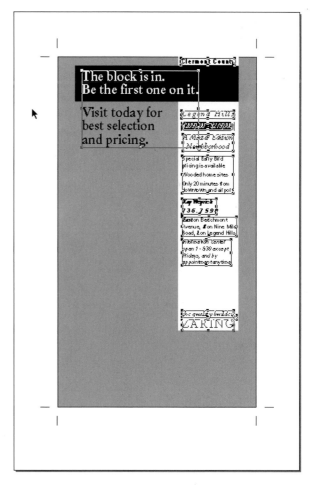

Next Fisher replaced the gray rectangle with the landscape photo, positioning it behind the rectangles and type. She cropped the photo with FreeHand's Paste Inside command: After drawing a rectangle the size the ad was going to run, she Cut the photo, then selected the rectangle and chose Paste Inside. After specifying a line of None for the rectangle, she was left with a perfectly cropped image.

STEP 6: DRAW CIRCLE

To create the circle around the house, Fisher simply drew it with FreeHand's circle tool. She gave it a fill of None and specified a white dotted line of 12-point width.

STEP 7: ADD PHOTO

She would use Paste Inside again to crop the house inside the circle, but she had to take another step first. FreeHand allocates the width of a specified stroke to both sides of a line—half on one side and half on the other—so in this case, the actual circle she had drawn ran through the center of the dotted line. If she'd pasted the photo inside that circle, it would have stuck out between the dots. To get the picture to stop at the inner edge of the dotted line, she had to clone the larger circle, specify no line, and shrink the new circle until it was even with the inside of the dashed line. Then she cut the house photo and pasted it inside the smaller circle. Last, she grouped the circles and moved them to line up the horizons on the two photos.

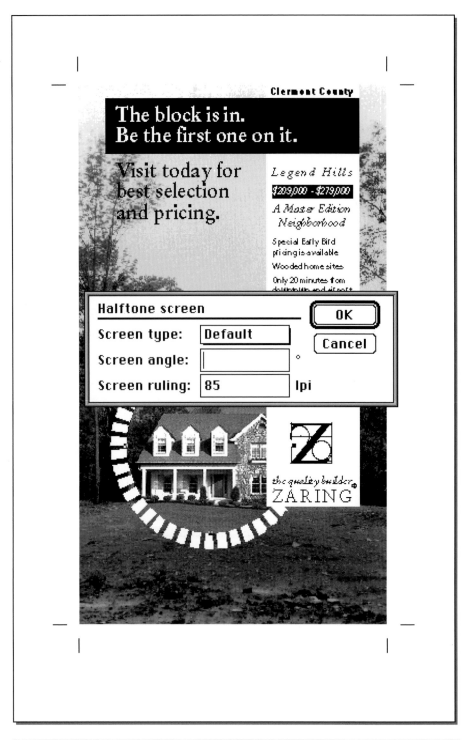

The final touch was to use FreeHand's Attributes menu to set the images' halftone screen. Fisher chose a dot screen at the default angle and 85 lpi, an appropriate halftone screen for newspaper reproduction. By using that command, she could be sure that changing printers, or settings in the Print dialog box, wouldn't affect the output.

GLOSSARY

Most of these terms have roots in the traditional techniques of publishing and design, but these definitions pertain solely to electronic design.

bitmap *or* **bitmapped graphic:** An image represented as a pattern of dots, whether black-and-white of varying shades and colors. Such graphics can include textural or painterly effects, but they take up much more disk space than *vector graphics* (see entry).

dither: A technique for representing a color by placing dots of related colors next to one another; for example, representing yellow-green by alternating dots of yellow and green. The technique is used when an output or display device, such as an inkjet printer or 8-bit monitor, is unable to accurately represent the full range of colors in an image.

em space: A horizontal measurement in typesetting, equal in width to the point size of the font in which the measurement is made.

en space: A horizontal measurement in type, equal in width to half an *em space* (see entry).

EPS (Encapsulated PostScript): A file format for graphics files combining the PostScript code that describes an image with a header that identifies it as a graphic, plus in most cases a preview image that lets you see the graphic on screen.

font: A single weight and style of a typeface. For instance, Times Roman is one font; Times Bold Italic is another. Also, the computer file containing the information required to reproduce the typeface.

FPO (For Position Only): A rough or limited version of a graphic used in the initial stages of a layout and later replaced with the final version.

halftone: A technique for representing the continuous tones of a photograph as a pattern of dots of varying sizes; also the term used for such a representation.

keyline: A thin line describing the boundary of a piece of art. Appearing on a mechanical, the keyline provides a guideline for stripping in the final art.

mechanical: A position (paper) version of a layout, usually printed on an imagesetter. The mechanical is photographed to make page film for printing.

moiré: An unwanted, visible pattern in a printed, color-separated image, caused by improper registration of the process color halftones.

PostScript: A programming language that provides a way to describe all the elements of a page—their size, placement, color, etc.—as well as the page itself. A PostScript printer driver translates page-layout information into PostScript code, and a PostScript printer interprets the code and renders the page.

process color: One of the four ink colors—cyan, magenta, yellow and black—which are printed in offset halftones to re-create the full range of colors in a printed photograph.

proof: A test version of a document that allows its creator to check for errors.

registration: The alignment of separate plates during printing. Usually refers to the effort to assure that the different colors of a color-separated page line up correctly.

reversed out: Printed as negative space—as empty space in the middle of an area of color—so that the paper shows through to delineate the text or the graphic.

sans serif: A style of typeface lacking the small finishing strokes, called *serifs*, on the stems of the characters.

scan: To convert an image or text to digital form as a bitmapped graphic by reading it with an electronic camera-like device—a scanner. Also, commonly, the file that results from that process.

screen: To reduce the saturation of a color by breaking it up into tiny dots. Varying the size and closeness of the dots allows the color to appear at fractions of its full intensity.

separate: To assign the individual colors on a page to their own printing plates. *Spot color separations*, most often used for flat color elements and type, place all the objects of a given color on the same plate. *Process color separations*, ordinarily used for photographic and other continuous-tone images, break down every element on the page into the same four process colors and put each one of those on a separate plate.

serif: A small finishing stroke on the stems of letters, for which one category of typeface designs is named.

spot color: A single color used in one defined area on a page, separated and printed as its own plate.

stripping: The process of adding separate elements—such as a halftoned photograph—into final page film by cutting holes in the page film and inserting the film for the added elements.

template: A prototype version of a document that serves as a basis for later versions, in which the template's design elements are replaced by the desired ones.

TIFF: A graphics file format for representing bitmapped images.

tracking: Adjustment of the space between letters in text.

trapping: A technique for preventing unwanted gaps between areas of printed color caused by bad registration. A *spread* is the increase in size of one color element so it overlaps an abutting one. A *choke* is the reduction in size of a gap or hole in one element so that an overlying element extends past the edges of the hole.

vector graphic: An image represented as a mathematical description—of its starting point, angle, length, etc. These graphics often have a hard-edged, pen-and-ink appearance and take up much less room on disk than a bitmapped graphic.

PERMISSIONS

pp. 2-9: ©1991 Light Source Computer Images, Inc. Used by permission of TonBo designs.

pp. 10-17: illustration ©1992 Valentin Sahleanu; brochure design ©1992 BHA Design Group. Used by permission of Valentin Sahleanu Design & Illustration.

pp. 18-25: cover photograph © Randolph Falk; report © Monica Ames Design. Used by permission of Monica Ames Design.

pp. 26-31: © Monica Ames Design. Used by permission of Monica Ames Design.

pp. 32-35: © Fisher & Day. Used by permission of Fisher & Day.

pp. 36-43: ©1993 The Black Point Group. Used by permission of The Black Point Group.

pp. 44-49: ©1992 Rainwater Design. Used by permission of Rainwater Design.

pp. 50-55: © TechArt San Francisco. Used by permission of TechArt San Francisco.

pp. 56-61: © TonBo designs. Used by permission of TonBo designs.

pp. 62-65: ©1992 Centre Reinsurance. Used by permission of WYD Design, Inc.

pp. 66-71: © Sharon L. Anderson and Johnathan Caponi. Used by permission of Sharon L. Anderson and Johnathan Caponi. Back panel photograph © Patrick Combs.

pp. 72-79: © David Salanitro Studio. Used by permission of David Salanitro Studio.

pp. 80-85: © Design North , Inc. Used by permission of Design North, Inc.

pp. 86-93: © P/R Design Group, Inc. Used by permission of P/R Design Group, Inc.

pp. 94-99: ©1992 OnLine Design Publications, Inc. Used by permission of Visual Strategies.

pp. 100-105: ©1992 Windham Hill Records. Used by permission of Visual Strategies.

pp.106-111: ©1992 California Alumni Association. Used by permission of Visual Strategies.

pp. 112-119: ©1992 DiVa Corporation. DiVa VideoShop is a trademark of DiVa Corporation. Used by permission of Imprimatur.

pp. 120-125: © Fisher & Day. Used by permission of Fisher & Day.

pp. 126-132: ©1993 Zender + Associates, Inc. Used by permission of Zender + Associates, Inc.

INDEX